THE VISION OF
FRANK
LLOYD
WRIGHT

RIGHT
**The John C. Pew House
(interior), Shorewood
Hills, Wisc. (1940)**

OPPOSITE
**The Frederick C. Robie
House, Chicago, Ill.
(1909)**

OVERLEAF
**Taliesin West, Scottsdale
Ariz. (1938)**

THE VISION OF
FRANK
LLOYD
WRIGHT

CHARTWELL
BOOKS, INC.

THOMAS A. HEINZ

Published in 2001 by
Chartwell Books, Inc.
A division of Book Sales, Inc.
Raritan Center
114 Northfield Avenue
Edison. NJ 08837 USA

Copyright © 2000 Regency House Publishing Ltd

ISBN 0-7858-1186-9

Printed in Hong Kong

CONTENTS

CHAPTER ONE
A Biography

This photograph was taken in about 1890. Young Frank is seated on the far right and sports a moustache. His wife, Catherine, is at the centre of the picture with their first-born, Frank Lloyd Wright Jnr., (better known as Lloyd). His mother, Anna Wright, is seated between them, and his uncle Jenkin Lloyd Jones and his wife are on the far left. Next to Catherine and Anna are two of Frank's sisters, while on the far right is a cousin

The Lloyd Jones family, Frank Lloyd Wright's ancestors on his mother's side, can be traced back to the hills of west Wales, where they were native to the area long before written records of the population were kept and where they continued to live well into the 17th century. They were hatters, and the story goes that a Lloyd Jones hat was a very durable object indeed. To prove the point, it is said that it could support a person standing on it without them falling off. No one is quite sure why this should be a test of a good hat, or how this durability was achieved, but it made for an amazing object and would certainly be of help to customers of small stature.

The ethics and morals of the people of this region seem to have been transmitted genetically to succeeding generations. They were extremely righteous and once a belief was firmly held believed it to be the basis for truth, and the conviction soon spread throughout the group. The motto by which they lived was and remains, 'Truth against the World'. They were Baptists and Calvinists and lived in the Cambrian District of Cardiganshire, also known as West Dyfed, around Llandysul. The Teifi river brought the

Frank Lloyd Wright photographed at Taliesin West around 1958, about a year before his death

William Russell Cary Wright, the father of Frank Lloyd Wright, photographed when he was a pastor at Weymouth, Massachusetts

goods of this area to the shores of Cardigan Bay, situated on the coast of the Irish Sea between Britain and Ireland. This was the area where the first Unitarians appeared and Jenkin Lloyd Jones had founded his own congregation by the 1720s in what was one of the least populated areas of the island.

Because of the mounting pressures placed on independent thinkers, they felt that it would be easier for them to seek a new and less restrictive location where they could peaceably live by their own rules. The first of them left Wales in the autumn of 1844 and set sail for New York. After what was always a difficult voyage across the Atlantic, they decided to push on across New York state, pausing in Ohio before finally settling in Ixonia, Wisconsin. Ixonia was and still is a small town of less than a thousand situated about halfway between Milwaukee and Madison.

Frank Lloyd Wright knew his grandfather and grandmother, Richard and Mallie Lloyd Jones. Of their 11 children, 6 made it to Ixonia and included Thomas born in 1830; John 1832; Margaret 1835; Mary 1836; Hanna (Frank's mother, later called Anna) 1838; Nanny 1840 (who died on the trip to Wisconsin); and Jenkin 1843. Once settled in their new home, Richard and Mallie had four more children, Elinor in 1845; Jane in 1848; James in 1850 and Enos in 1853.

In 1846 the family purchased two 40-acre

(16-hectare) parcels of land from the government for $1.25 an acre and continued to buy land until they had acquired 110 acres which they sold for $3.50 an acre when they moved further west to Iowa county. In 1856 Richard and his family moved from Ixonia and tried their hand at farming in Bear Creek and then Lone Rock, by April 1864 finally settling in what was to become known as the Jones Valley at an elbow on the left bank of the Wisconsin river. All together, they owned 1,800 acres (720 hectares) of a valley which was quite fertile and bordered by small hills on three sides. Each member acquired expertise in a wide range of skills – all essential to a pioneer lifestyle. They all knew how to make something from nothing – how to use their imagination to create useful things. Thomas became the unschooled but much practised architect and builder for the family and many other clients; John was a farmer and the mill he built and the grain he produced supplied the family and others in the area. Margaret and Mary both got married and left, and Jenkin fought in the Civil War and became a devotee of President Abraham Lincoln. He returned to become a preacher after attending college at Meadville, Pennsylvania, while Elinor (or Nell, as she was known), became a teacher, as did Jane who went to Minneapolis to pursue her studies. Together, Nell and Jane, who never

Anna Lloyd Jones, the mother of Frank LLoyd Wright

married, founded the Hillside Home School within the family valley, while James was a farmer and the last, Enos, only 14 years older than Frank Lloyd Wright, started in college but was unable to finish because of lack of funds. His farm was the smallest.

There were seven farms in all and each had its own distinctive farmhouse. Most of the siblings could see one another's houses from their windows but were not close enough to lack privacy and they were scattered in random fashion throughout the landscape. A hamlet developed at the south-west end of the valley had its own post office and was known as Hillside. Enos' farm was across the road to the south of what would be the Hillside Home School building, while Thomas', the builder, was located just west of the school. James' farm was at the far east end of the valley, east of the chapel and cemetery where the road turns to the south.

Hanna Lloyd Jones later became known as Anna. Like her two younger sisters, Nell and Jane, she was a teacher, and had an abiding interest in education. She had been born and had spent her early years in Wales and Welsh was her first language; she appears to have had a difficult time learning English and had developed her own method of phonetic spelling. She spoke with an accent, as many at the time did, and she was tough and more than willing to take under her wing anyone willing to learn and who desired to

better themselves. She rarely fell off a horse, perhaps because she was so tenacious, but was not a warm person or one with whom one could share intimacies.

The one factor that made all of them so tough was that Mallie Lloyd Jones taught each of her children the lore of the flowers, plants and animals which surrounded them and which consequently made them so at home in the valley. She considered that they would feel more comfortable if they knew how they fitted in with the scheme of things and how they could utilize the resources at hand. Inspired by the family motto, 'Truth Against the World', she taught her children, and in turn their children, to appreciate truth, beauty, nature and simplicity.

William Russell Cary Wright meets Anna Lloyd Jones

Curiously, the date and circumstances of the courtship and marriage of Anna Lloyd Jones and William Russell Cary Wright were never recorded. William Wright had been married before to Permilia Holcomb in the mid-1850s and they had had three children, Charles William Wright, George Irving Wright and Elizabeth Amelia Wright. Permilia died in 1863, the same year the Lloyd Joneses and Anna were living in Lone Rock. Anna was still a spinster at 28 and a teacher who visited the homes of pupils rather than having them assembled in an expensive schoolhouse.

Teachers, at that time, often lodged at their pupils' homes for days or weeks at a time before moving on to the next.

Anna and William may have met through their professions, for William Wright was the superintendent of the school district and would have had to have certified each teacher's credentials and oversee their assignments in order for them to receive their salaries. He was 14 years older than Anna and she seemed very happy at the prospect of the marriage.

William Wright was a fine fellow, gave a powerful first impression and made friends easily, though friendships were not always consolidated because he was often on the move. His talents were wide-ranging: he had studied law and was a commissioner of the Richland County Circuit Court, taught music and several instruments, and wrote and published songs and music. He had a fine bass voice, was a memorable speaker, and in time was ordained as a Baptist minister.

The Wrights – William, Anna and the three children of Wright's first marriage, moved to Richland Center from Lone Rock, less than 20 miles to the north-west, when Anna was eight months pregnant with their first child, and where William was to supervise the Central Baptist Society's new building. The exact location of their residence is not recorded but it is there that on 8 June 1867 Frank Lloyd Wright was born.

OPPOSITE
The Jones Valley, Wisconsin, the home of the large Lloyd Jones family, where they established their farms and at last began to lead a settled life

Anna idolized her son, and right from the start decided that he was destined to become an architect. Many regarded this as sheer fantasy, that she could have predetermined her son's future profession; but there are images of Gothic cathedrals taken from *Harper's Weekly* in Taliesin's archives which Anna is said to have hung in her son's nursery as a portent of what he would later become.

Flight of the Wrights

The Wrights did not remain long in Richland Center. Before young Frank could talk, they had moved to McGregor, Iowa in March 1869. McGregor was downriver of the Jones Valley, where the Wisconsin river joins the Mississippi on the right bank, and has not changed much in the years since the Wrights first arrived. The town is situated in a cleft of the stone bluffs alongside the river which are quite tall and as a result shield much of the town from direct sun for several months of the year. Again, Anna was eight months pregnant, this time with Mary Jane, or Jennie as she would be known.

While the townspeople appeared satisfied with their new pastor, William Wright was not in fact very proficient at raising money for the building and operation of the new Baptist Society, though he seemed to be good at just about everything else. It follows, therefore, that it was money, or the lack of it, that plagued him for the rest of his life, and which

caused all the trauma and upheaval in his second marriage.

A few years later, and after a short period spent on the family farms in the Jones Valley, in 1873 the Wrights moved on to Pawtucket, Rhode Island and the High Street Baptist Church. The community, of course, was in need of funds to rebuild the church that had burned down three years earlier, but William was also required to raise money to get the congregation out of debt. The Wright family did not live in Pawtucket but in a little town further uphill called Central Falls, a stone's throw from the Massachusetts state line.

Apparently, William was not able to raise enough money even to pay his own salary and by December 1873, the Wrights were forced to admit defeat and moved to William's father's house in Essex, Connecticut. After a period of recuperation, they were again ready to move by September 1874, and arrived at Weymouth, Massachusetts and the First Baptist Church, which is just south of Boston on the bay and adjacent to Braintree. Frank was by now old enough for school and they found him one in Weymouth; but his father's new venture also seemed to be running out of steam and the Wrights moved yet again, and by 1877 were back in Wisconsin. William had obtained the position of pastor at the Liberal Church, a Unitarian establishment in Wyoming, near to the Jones Valley.

Anna's brother, Jenkin Lloyd Jones, had

completed his religious studies and had by now progressed up the ranks of the Unitarian ministry. He was located in Chicago on the fashionable south side and founded a parish at 39th Street and Langley Boulevard where his ministry was based on progressive rather than traditional teaching. In about 1885 he decided to hire an architect new to Chicago, Joseph Lyman Silsbee, who was known for the 'Shingle Style' of residential design.

The church was known as **All Souls** and resembled a large house rather than a Gothic cathedral, with the auditorium on the second floor and many smaller rooms for other activities of interest to the congregation. Jenkin befriended other progressive thinkers in Chicago and its environs and these included William C. Gannet of Hinsdale and Frances Willard of Evanston. Gannet was the editor of a magazine, *Unity*, while Willard was an advocate of temperance and founded the WCTU, the Women's Christian Temperance Union, which still has its headquarters in Evanston. Not many years ago, Evanston voted to allow liquor to be sold and served for the first time.

The following year, Jenkin hired Silsbee to produce a design for a small chapel for the Jones Valley. It was to be constructed by his brother Thomas and located to the centre of the south end of the valley between James' and Enos' farms. Known as the **Unity Chapel**, it was to have a family cemetery

All Souls Church, Chicago, Ill. (1885)
On the left of the picture is the Lincoln Center while on the right is All Souls Church, designed by Joseph Lyman Silsbee for Jenkin Lloyd Jones. The following year, Silsbee was also asked to design a small place of worship for the Jones Valley, which was called the Unity Chapel

The Unity Chapel, Spring Green, Wisc. (1886)

The architect of this chapel was, again, Joseph Lyman Silsbee and it is thought that the young Frank Lloyd Wright was allowed to help him on the project although it is uncertain what his duties were. However, the experience was enough to awaken the young man's interest in architecture and he never looked back

adjacent to it. When the design for the chapel was published, however, reference was made to a young boy assistant. The only candidate to fit this description was Frank who would have met Silsbee through his Uncle Jenkin in the course of the chapel's design and construction; this was Frank's first

contact with an established architect, and guaranteed to fire his interest in the subject.

At the age of 55, William Wright was again making a new start in a new location. He was apparently feeling invigorated and had some money for he opened his Conservatory of Music on Pickney Street in

Madison. He and the family went to live in a house they bought at Gorham and Livingston and to which they made some improvements. The house was a one-and-a-half-storey frame building in a district near to the State Capitol on the isthmus between Lake Mendota and Lake Monona.

It is curious that in every place where he had ever lived, from the time that he could walk, Frank Lloyd Wright had been within walking distance of a navigable body of water. Given this association, there usually develops an affinity with boating, sailing or fishing, but Frank had no interest in water whatsoever.

Divorce

This outward appearance of contentment and prosperity must have been short-lived, for Anna Wright decided to withdraw from her husband and they began to sleep in different rooms. William protested, but to no avail, and soon felt that his only recourse was to terminate the marriage, filing for a divorce in the summer of 1884. The couple decided on a settlement: Anna and the children would get the house in its entirety, while William would take his clothing and a few minor possessions and depart, leaving Anna and her children to be supported by her family, the Lloyd Joneses. There is no evidence that Anna ever worked at an outside job to provide income for her family and it must

have been burdensome for them to maintain her in her house in Madison, 30 miles (48km) from the rest of the family.

Little is recorded concerning the activities of young Frank. He had been surrounded by music when his father had been present and this interest continued throughout his life. He had learned to play the piano and had a good knowledge of other classical instruments.

Because the family had moved about so much, Frank was unable to develop any friendships he had made until he moved to Madison. Perhaps he felt inadequate with the popular set, but he befriended Robert Lamp who had lost both legs to polio and had to walk supported on crutches. Robert lived close by to the Wrights and they got along well, both being creative, Frank with his hands and Robie with his imaginative ideas. Together they became interested in printing and printing presses, and when they managed to acquire one began producing any number of things. It is unfortunate that none of these appear to have survived, even in mother Anna's carefully maintained files.

University, then Chicago

Frank's academic achievements were average and there is no evidence that he graduated from high school. Although his grades may not have been outstanding, it is obvious that he learned a great deal when one looks at

what he was able to accomplish later on. Somehow, he was admitted as a special student to an engineering course at the University of Wisconsin, the campus of which was within walking distance of his house in Madison. It was not like going off to school in some remote location and in order to help pay his fees and perhaps to assist with the household expenses, he got a job with the head of the engineering school, Allan D. Connover.

As well as being academically unexceptional, Frank was also an inconsistent student and missed much of his schooling. He attended classes at the beginning and end of 1886 but decided to leave Madison to seek his fortune as an architect in Chicago. It was a bold move and one that had been planned for some time. Frank purloined a few of his mother's possessions – her mink collar and fine books – and pawned them for travel and a little pocket money once he arrived.

He describes his first days, alone in Chicago, when he visits a series of architectural offices and names them. The details that he gave in his 1928 recollection are very reliable and the route he took can be easily plotted from office to office; there was little backtracking. He also recounts seeing a show in an Adler & Sullivan theatre. In researching the dates this play appeared in Chicago, it appears he arrived

RIGHT
Frank Lloyd Wright and his
friend and mentor Cecil
Corwin

OPPOSITE
**Hillside Home School,
Jones Valley, Wisc.
(1887)**
This was the first of Frank
Lloyd Wright's designs and
was built by his uncle. It
stood to the east of the
present Hillside building in
the Jones Valley at Taliesin

about six months earlier than has previously
been reported and this lends credence to the
reassessment and earlier date when combined
with the completion of his uncle's Silsbee-
designed church, All Souls, which he claims
to have seen to the end of its construction.

Encouraged by his uncle Jenkin Lloyd
Jones and on the strength of his small
experience of architecture when he worked
with Joseph Lyman Silsbee on the Unity
Chapel, Frank decided to ask Silsbee for a
job, to which he agreed, and he went to
work in the architect's Chicago office. John
Waterman had a son, Harry, who was an
architect who also worked at Silsbee's. It was
therefore quite convenient for Frank to lodge
with the Waterman family in Vincennes Street,
around the corner from Jenkin Lloyd Jones'
All Souls church on 39th Street.

For some reason, this arrangement lasted
for only a few months and Frank returned
to Madison and to classes at the University.
However, he only managed to last through
to the end of the term and decided to return
to Chicago in the spring of 1887. He decided
he could do better without further studies
and applied and was accepted into the
office of Beers, Clay & Dutton. Frank admits
himself that the job was beyond him but he
was fortunately able to talk himself back
into Silsbee's office. The drafting-room
manager at Silsbee's was a young man
named Cecil Corwin.

Cecil Corwin and his Pal Frank

According to Wright's autobiography, Corwin and Frank got along famously and, unable or unwilling to submit to academic training, Wright claimed he was being educated at 'Cecil College' where he was learning more about life than at any stuffy educational establishment. He learned to appreciate Chicago through his close association with Corwin and they visited the theatre, dined in fine and not so fine restaurants, and attended art exhibitions and lectures together.

The two were constant companions even though Corwin was seven years older than Wright. Perhaps the attraction Corwin had for Wright was his academic training and the exotic locations that he had seen before arriving in Chicago and living with his brother, an artist, on the near west side.

Silsbee's office contained other talented people who would go on to greater things on their own account. One was George Grant Elmslie and another George Washington Maher, and it is possible that early influences make lasting impressions for both Elmslie and Maher continued their careers in Silsbee's line of residential design.

Wright learned very quickly and was already producing renderings of smaller projects for the office. These appeared in the distinguished journal, *Inland Architect*, in March and May 1888 and although they were hardly distinguished works of art and were

RIGHT and OPPOSITE
Adler & Sullivan's
Auditorium Building,
Chicago, 1886–89

not the largest or best designs to have come from Silsbee's office, they were nevertheless published.

While Wright was employed by Silsbee on a full-time basis, he began outside work almost immediately. Wright's design for a residential-type school building in 1887 for his aunts, Nell and Jane, was built by his uncle Thomas in the Jones Valley. It resembled an oversized house and was named the **Hillside Home School** and was a boarding school for children at elementary and high school levels. Through his uncle's connections, Frank also designed a fantasy house for Henry Cooper who was a neighbour of Jenkin's friend, William C. Gannet, also of Hinsdale.

Jenkin came to the rescue again when Anna, Frank's mother, decided she must live nearer to her son. A Unitarian minister who was under Jenkin's charge, Augusta Chapin, took in the entire Wright family which included Frank's two sisters, Anna and Frank. Chapin's house was located on Forest Avenue in west suburban Oak Park.

At Adler & Sullivan
With two renderings published under his own name as draftsman and a building of his own design under construction, Wright must have felt he was outgrowing residential work and was beginning to search for greater opportunities. With this in mind, he went

Catherine (Kitty) Tobin, Frank Lloyd Wright's first wife. They were married on 1 June 1889 when she was just 18 and Frank was 22

looking for a position at the most progressive and modern architectural office in Chicago, that of Adler & Sullivan. When introducing himself as a design talent, it is likely that it was Louis Sullivan himself who conducted the interview. Wright said he was familiar with the abstract ornamentation produced by Sullivan who in turn asked to see some of Wright's work of this type as well as other designs. Apparently caught out in a lie, Wright went home and worked overnight to produce some new work and included the Cooper design and the Silsbee renderings. Sullivan may not have been impressed with the work, but he was certainly impressed with the man and hired Wright in late 1887.

Sullivan needed extra hands to assist him in completing work on a new, very large building for the Chicago lake-front, the **Auditorium Building**. This was a revolutionary concept, one of the first multi-use structures, and was to include a hotel, a set of offices and a large performance hall.

Cecil Corwin must have also felt as though he could improve his position and by 1888 was in partnership with office colleague George W. Maher. There are a few published accounts of their collaboration but it apparently did not last for more than four years, leaving Corwin on his own; but few published notices or buildings appeared in the architectural press. He was, however, able to secure a large commission for the

growing medical facility on the near west side, the Rush Medical School. Corwin also designed a house for his brother, his father and himself nearby, though no photographs of it have come to light.

Wright must have come to the conclusion that he was doing well financially for, on his 21st birthday, he bought a piece of vacant land three blocks north of Reverend Chapin's house in Oak Park, purchasing it from a long-time Oak Park resident and real estate broker, E.O. Gale. There was much speculation in property circles all over the Chicago area but Oak Park was an especially vibrant market. S.S. Beman and his wife, the architect of the Pullman Palace Car Company, was also speculating in Oak Park and on the same block as Wright's property. Gale financed the project for Wright

Wright thought he knew something about handling money and must have had some because about a year later he bought an empty lot on the opposite corner of his first purchase from a Scottish landscape gardener, John Blair, who had moved some time earlier to Colorado Springs and finally to British Columbia in Canada. His mother bought the eastern half of the same lot a few months later and moved into the Victorian frame cottage. Frank who had by then married Kitty Tobin moved in with her and Frank's sister, which caused a certain amount of tension between the women. It is unclear how Anna

was able to afford such a purchase for she is reputed to have been as poor as a church mouse all her adult life.

Frank had met Catherine Tobin at his uncle's church and it was the Reverend Jones who performed their wedding ceremony. They soon began having children – six in all: Frank Lloyd junior, John, Catherine, Frances, David and Robert. The eldest two eventually followed their father's profession, also ignoring academic training for apprenticeships. They both worked for their father, Lloyd being associated with Frank for over 20 years. John was a less distinguished architectural designer and is perhaps better known for his invention of a children's toy, Lincoln Logs.

Wright had been able to build his first house by obtaining a $5,000 loan from one of his employers, Louis Sullivan, and the agreement for it was drawn up by a Sullivan client, Mr. Felsenthall. Again, contrary to popular opinion, there were no provisions for prohibiting additional work being undertaken outside Frank's terms of employment with Adler & Sullivan. Indeed, it would have been to Sullivan's advantage if Wright was making extra money as he would have been able to pay the loan back more rapidly. There were provisions for monthly payments of the principal and interest as with any large loan and Sullivan must have had great faith in the young Wright to have trusted him thus.

Wright claims he was hired to work on the Auditorium Building and on several others in the five years he was at Adler & Sullivan's offices, which were relocated to the tower of the Auditorium. Wright also worked on drawings for the Illinois Central station in New Orleans, Sullivan's brother, Albert, being a vice-President of the railroad. Adler & Sullivan also designed several train stations in Chicago for the Illinois Central Railroad.

Both Adler and Sullivan took their work most seriously and approached it in a businesslike manner. Their intention was to make money doing what they were good at and, because of this commitment, they assessed the best method for practising their business as architects. They found that there were bigger profits in large commercial buildings than in residences and as a result decided to avoid commissions for houses. In spite of this rule, they were obligated through business associations to execute some, however, and it would appear that Sullivan, the chief designer, brought Wright in to assist in the design and execution of at least a few of which the **Charnley House** on Chicago's near north side seems to be the best example. The design builds on Sullivan's initial ideas and simplifies them, as Wright would do in his own work later on.

As it turned out, Frank made very few repayments of his loan, for when he left his employment with Adler & Sullivan, he had to

pay $5,700 back. At this time there was very little work in the office, there were now fewer than five employees, and Dankmar Adler had decided to retire; in fact the national economy was in a state of depression, so it was reasonable to suppose that Wright would soon be out of a job. Fortunately, he did have independent work. He had just won a competition to design two boathouses in his home town of Madison, one of which was built, though the money for the construction of the other was never realized.

Once Wright was his own man, he returned to familiar territory. He began to associate again with his friend, Cecil Corwin, though Wright was quick to emphasize that it was not a partnership. They took offices in an Adler & Sullivan building, the Garrick Theater, near to where the Silsbee offices were located, employing a few draftsmen from time to time. A few house designs came Wright's way while Corwin was finishing work on the Rush Medical building. Unfortunately, Corwin was dissatisfied with the arrangement and went on to have an undistinguished career in New York, not marrying until his 60s.

First Independent Work

Wright claims that he designed several impressive houses while working with Adler & Sullivan, maintaining that in order to conceal his outside work from his employers, they were noted and published under the

OPPOSITE and LEFT
The James Charnley House, Chicago, Ill. (1891)
This was thought to have been designed by Wright while employed by Adler & Sullivan since the practice was dedicated to large commercial buildings and theatres. It is now the national headquarters for the Society of Architectural Historians

name of his friend, Cecil Corwin. It is stretching the imagination to think that an older, independent architect such as Corwin would be unable to get a job where a much younger, inexperienced man succeeded. Moreover, it would have been difficult for Wright while working full-time to oversee construction while meeting clients in secrecy. Corwin had had better and longer training than Wright and it would make more sense to suppose that the commissions were Corwin's and that Wright had merely assisted.

After leaving the Adler & Sullivan offices, Wright's first independent commission was for a very large and costly house for a supplier of materials to Adler & Sullivan, William Winslow, of the Winslow Brothers Iron Works. The house was of golden iron-spot Roman brick construction with a large plaster frieze surrounding the second floor. Looking at the Winslow house now, one cannot imagine the ridicule that Winslow received from his neighbours for building such a wildly modern and exotic house.

Early Work and Clients

Wright was one of the best salesmen of all time and was able to convince a great many well-to-do, independent-minded industrialists to hire him to design houses for them in the Chicago area. Wright's earliest work was not astonishing but improved rapidly; most of his work was for his Oak Park neighbours who

were so pleased with the results that they helped convince their family and business associates to make use of Wright's services as well.

William Winslow, obviously impressed, decided to hire Wright as architectural consultant for a new venture. The Luxfer Prism Company was about to change the shape of architecture by providing prism glass that would bring much needed light into buildings and this new product was enthusiastically embraced by all the major Chicago architects. Wright designed many of these 4-inch square (10cm²) prism plates for the company, though only a very few were used. What Wright received for this work provided him with enough money to allow him to build a working studio onto the north side of his 1889 Oak Park house while continuing to maintain a downtown Chicago office where he could meet corporate clients. The office in 1897 was next door to the Luxfer Prism offices in a building owned by Winslow's neighbour and Wright's client, Edward C. Waller.

Although Wright had attended few university classes and had never enrolled in a formal architectural programme, he liked to hire associates who were well educated and the people who became prominent in his office and afterwards, such as Marion Mahony, all successfully completed their studies. Mahony was the second woman to graduate from Massachusetts Institute of Technology and Walter Burley Griffin and William Drummond were from the University of Illinois programme run by Nathan C. Ricker in Urbana, Illinois. As in any architectural practice, there were a whole string of workers; some designers, some engineering-oriented, and there were draftsmen and renderers. There was always a need for office and managerial assistance and this seemed to fall to another woman architect, Isabel Roberts.

Wright also worked with artists able to take on board his own ideas and incorporate them into the fabric and texture of a building. One of his associates was Richard Bock who used Wright's downtown office as well as his Oak Park studio for modelling his sculptures. Bock was also an architectural client.

Oak Park

Oak Park was and remains a fashionable suburb of Chicago. It is easily accessible to Chicago's Loop or central business district by good roads and two train systems. With many clients in the neighbourhood, Wright's life was bound to them not only on a professional level but also on a social plane. Within several blocks of Wright's house were two other families who would become prominent figures; they included Edgar Rice Burroughs, the inventor of the Tarzan books, and another literary figure lived even closer and attended school with Wright's children, Ernest Hemingway. It was also at this time that Wright became interested in Japan, its art, lifestyle, customs and food.

Wright was now able to keep longer hours and meet his residential clients in the evenings, as still happens, by having his workplace built onto his house, which also exposed his family to his work. The Wrights threw exotic parties that were reported in the local newspapers and according to Wright there were times when there were parties going on all through his house and studio. His success brought him into contact with many progressive thinkers of the time, including Clarence Darrow, Elbert Hubbard, Jane Addams, Sherwood Anderson, Frances Browne, and Frank Baum, who were all within his circle of friends and acquaintances.

It was fashionable and not too unusual for people in his position to go on an extended European trip to take in the great architecture, art and music of Europe. It was especially true of architects to take the 'Grand Tour' which included England, France, Italy and Greece to

OPPOSITE
The Luxfer Prism Company Skyscraper, Chicago, Ill. (1897)
Proposed office building design. Wright was hired by the company as its architectural consultant and the drawing was intended to show the potential use of the new glazing product. (left). The company was founded by two Wright clients, Edward Waller and William Winslow

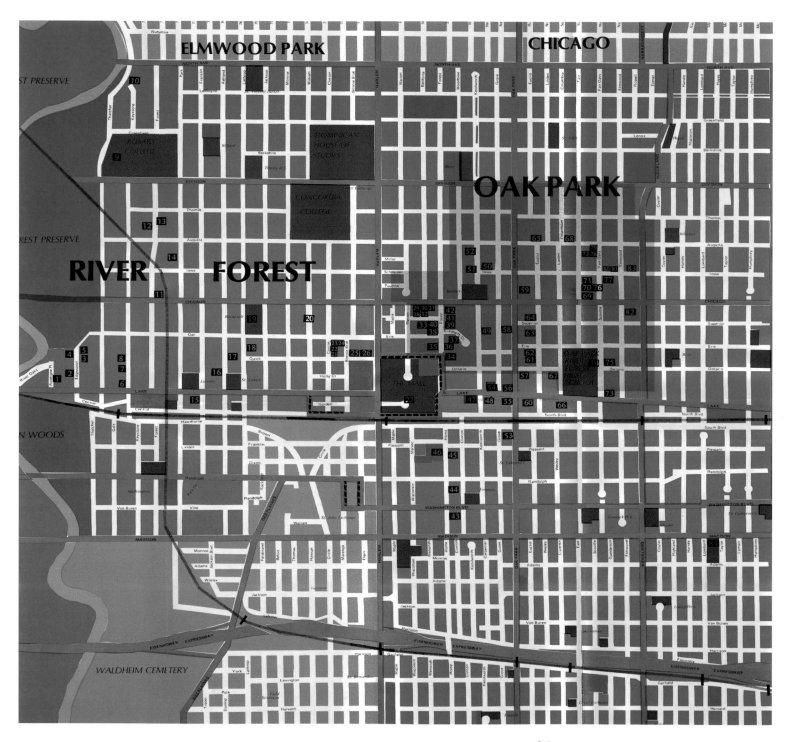

study the great historic buildings first-hand. This was to enable them to develop a greater understanding of classical styles and devices that might later influence their work in their own architectural practices. Wright, of course, discounted any possibility of there being any European influence in his work or any other aspect of his life and went instead in the opposite direction, to Japan, which he and his wife visited with clients, the Ward Willits. They were gone for several months in 1905 and visited many of the most popular tourist attractions as well as a variety of unusual locations. The trip was memorable and celebrated in an album of photographs which has recently been published.

Wright had already absorbed much of his understanding of Japanese buildings and the trip did not alter his designs in any profound sense. He had been using simple surfaces and had already given up using the upturned roofs, reminiscent of historic Japanese houses and temples, in his own designs.

Floundering

Wright was so successful at getting clients that he had almost reached the point of having too much work. It is difficult to understand how, with his small staff, he could have produced the quantity as well as maintaining the quality of work – but he did. He would not only produce the design for the building at a new level of detail unusual in his day, but also intricate plans for art glass and furniture designs. It was not so much that the designs were completed but, because of their new and unusual nature, he also needed to educate the glass-maker and furniture producer, which was even more time-consuming.

All was not perfect, however. Wright also managed to lose some very large and important projects for major clients. Harold McCormick of the International Harvester Company of Chicago wanted an enormous house on the shore of Lake Michigan in the wealthiest suburb of Lake Forest, the drawings of which prefigured Wright's own country estate of Taliesin but on a larger and more formal scale. Henry Ford, the automobile manufacturer, also requested a large residence   both commissions were lost. Wright began to look for other diversions. He was not finding his work completely satisfying even though it was the period of some of his greatest innovations.

Mamah Borthwick Cheney

August 1908 was the date set for a fateful trip to Madison, Wisconsin, when the Wrights and their clients, Edwin and Mamah Cheney, drove up to visit Frank's boyhood friend and client, Robert Lamp. They visited a tiny

OPPOSITE

Plan of Oak Park, Illinois

BELOW

Projected drawing (1907) of a house for Harold McCormick of the International Harvester Company of Chicago, which was never realized

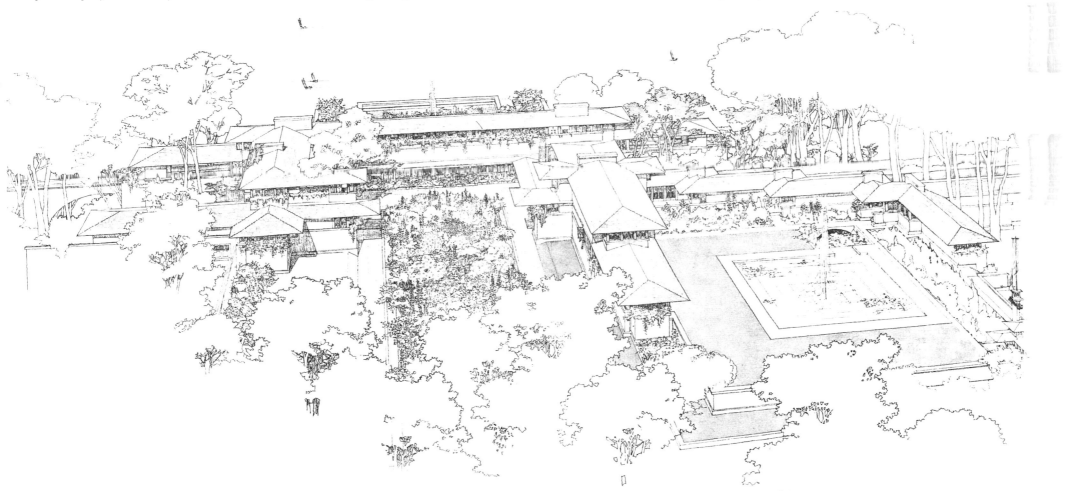

Mamah Borthwick Cheney
in 1911

private island, Rocky Roost, in Lake Mendota, that is not long since gone, and this was probably not the only common experience they enjoyed after the completion of the Cheney house in Oak Park.

Wright had contemplated a European trip for some time and decided to contact competent friends and associates willing to assume his work in his absence when they would also be given the use of his studio facilities. There were no takers until Herman von Holst allowed himself to be persuaded. The provisions of the contract were spelled out on paper and there was a stipulation for a thorough accounting on Wright's return.

Historically, the emphasis of this trip has been placed on the affair Wright was having with Mamah Borthwick Cheney. It is true that they met in New York after she had left her children in Colorado and he his wife, family and office in Oak Park. They travelled by boat and eventually arrived in Berlin in 1909 where they were discovered by the *Chicago Tribune* which announced the affair with lurid headlines. Wright was in Berlin to consult his publisher, Wasmuth, who was intending to produce a major portfolio of Wright's drawings together with a smaller book of photographs of his work.

During the period the couple were out of the country, however, they were actually together for less than half of the time for, after the first year, in September 1910, Wright

decided to return to Oak Park to arrange for his oldest son, Lloyd, and the son of a neighbour to meet and work with him on the drawings at a rented villa just outside Florence in the small village of Fiesole.

Meanwhile, Mamah Cheney was travelling in Sweden and probably taught languages for a time at the University of Leipzig in Germany, while Wright travelled with his son to Paris and later to Vienna with Mamah. In letters to a few close friends it is clear that Wright was in a state of considerable conflict over the matter of abandoning his family.

When he finally returned to Oak Park, however, his wife Catherine took him back without question, while Edwin Cheney initiated an uncontested divorce and Mamah reverted to her maiden name. She was allowed to see and travel with her children while Cheney remained in his Wright-designed house for 15 more years. He married a year and a day after the divorce became final, the first legal opportunity to do so, and the wedding took place in Detroit.

Wright had purchased land in the Jones Valley from members of his mother's family with the intention of building a country house and studio for himself. The initial drawings describe it as a building for his mother, perhaps to conceal his plans from his wife and office colleagues. The construction for it was under way soon after his return and he spent some time at Spring Green supervising

the work. He was to name this house and studio Taliesin, in a tribute to his Welsh ancestry.

Back to Chicago

Architecture is a very public profession: the work of an architect stands there on the street for all to see. One might have expected a scandal such as Wright had caused to have been detrimental to the career of a figure who was becoming a celebrity. This was not the case. Wright was supported by some of his most important clients – Little, Martin and Coonley – and several new clients appeared who had either not heard of or did not care about the scandal. They included Sherman Booth, an attorney, and his brother-in-law, Angster, and even a preacher from Kentucky, the Reverend Jessie Zeigler.

One client who had the potential to provide a considerable income for Wright was Arthur Richards of Milwaukee, who commissioned a hotel for Lake Geneva and proposed a new system for construction using pre-cut lumber. This was called the American Ready-Cut System in which each component was numbered according to its position on the blueprint. There were many building sizes in this scheme, from bungalows to multi-story duplexes, and each size had several options for doors, windows, bays and roofs. Richards was setting up a series of dealers to help sell this system, while Wright produced a great many drawings for these designs and over a dozen of them were built, most of which are in Milwaukee and the Chicago Metro area. Because of the advent of the First World War, they were not as successful as anticipated.

Mamah died in tragic circumstances in 1914 at Taliesin. Not only had she and her children been brutally murdered, the building had also been set on fire. A devastated Frank Lloyd Wright raised this memorial to her

American Systems Prefabricated Buildings (1916)

Arthur Richards of Milwaukee devised a system for using pre-cut lumber in construction which was known as the American Ready-Cut System which Wright incorporated into his designs

In 1913, another large commission came Wright's way through his earliest client, Winslow. The project was for an outdoor entertainment centre for Chicago's south side. Midway Gardens was to be constructed several blocks from the Robie house on land used 20 years earlier for the Columbian Exposition and World Fair of 1893.

Wright now had the opportunity of designing a complete complex for public use, rather than a private family house. The open-air theatre was to be the largest feature, along with an inside restaurant and other galleries, and Wright was to design the building, the furniture, lighting, the chinaware and the decorative elements of sculpture and wall panels.

It was while Wright and his second son John were at the site in the summer of 1914 that the news of a terrible tragedy reached them. On 14 August, a servant had served lunch to Mamah, her two children and several draftsmen and other workers. He then proceeded to spread gasoline around the outside of the dining room, locking all but one door. He then set the fire and as all were attempting to escape, ran amok with a machete. Realizing what was happening, several draftsmen leaped from the high windows, some in flames, and fell to the ground, their bones broken.

Wright and John were notified by telephone and left immediately for Taliesin where they met Edwin Cheney at the Chicago train station who was also on his way to the site. When they arrived, major portions of Taliesin had been burnt to the ground and there were several deaths including those of Mamah, the children and the servant by his own hand. No one knows what prompted his horrifying action. Wright requested that he alone bury the body of Mamah and chose a site in the family cemetery at the south end of the Jones Valley. He included bundles of fresh flowers as he closed the grave. What he had anticipated, after surviving several years of personal criticism for his actions, was a quiet life with the women he loved and the shock of this sudden and gruesome loss is not difficult to imagine. Many considered it to be God's way of repaying Wright for his transgressions and that it served him right.

Wright received a flood of letters as a result of all the publicity, one of which

particularly struck him and to which he decided to respond. It was from a divorced woman who described herself as an artist; they met within months and began living together soon after. Miriam Noel was an unusual choice of partner for Wright – in fact she was untypical of the women with whom he had earlier been associated. The relationship between Wright and Miriam Noel was a turbulent one. Wright was not yet divorced from his first wife, Catherine, and would not be until November 1922. Before they were married, Miriam Noel had accompanied Wright on trips to Japan but when he fell ill, it was his mother, Anna, who went over in 1920 to attend to his well-being, which made Miriam even more difficult to deal with. It appeared that Miriam was under the impression that she could exert influence on Wright and his work. This was not to be the case. By law, parties could not remarry for a year after a divorce and Wright married Miriam Noel in November 1923. Reading about it and judging from our own perspective it would have seemed the wrong thing for Wright to have done and apparently it was. Wright said, 'Marriage resulted in ruin for us both. Instead of improving with marriage, as I had hoped, our relationship became worse.' Once wed, their personal life became intolerable and they spent less and less time together. Miriam left Wright in April 1924 but did not divorce him immediately.

Taliesin, Spring Green, Wisc.

Taliesin is shown here in its 1925 evolution, having been damaged in two fires since its beginnings in 1911

Taliesin

Setting up his residence and his architectural practice in the country meant a dramatic change in the manner in which Wright was to proceed with his business. Future clients would of necessity have to be serious in their intentions as a consultation would have to be arranged long in advance and considerable effort would have to be expended by one of the parties to even get to the meeting. This meant that Wright was more likely to choose clients with larger projects or greater means. Many clients were loath to correspond with someone so distant via mail and the telephone was not popular for architectural discussions at that time.

It would also be more difficult to find workers who could assist in the execution of Wright's designs. However, Wright had some positive points on his side: he was well published and was now obtaining clients from further afield. He was no longer a neighbourhood architect or one associated with a single city, Chicago. He was also coming to be recognized on a national scale which would soon become international.

The First World War and After

The First World War and the decade following had seen a tremendous increase in personal wealth across America. With a taste for Europe, and having been taught that all things European were superior to those American, a change in attitude occurred and American design began to assume European influences. This spelled death to what Wright had achieved in the preceding 30 years and for all those who espoused indigenous American design.

While working on the Midway Gardens project, Wright's knowledge and interest in Japanese art and culture helped him when he was invited to negotiate for the design of a large hotel for the Japanese Imperial family. The site was an important one, across from the Imperial Palace. It was intended for visitors from the West, with all the amenities expected, but with Eastern influences superimposed. Wright was the perfect choice and developed a good relationship with the hotel manager and other hotel board members. This one commission lead to at least nine others for Japanese clients. The Imperial Hotel project lasted from 1914–1922.

On the day of the opening ceremonies of the Imperial Hotel, Japan was hit by one of the worst disasters in its history, the Kanto earthquake, which destroyed Tokyo and other nearby major cities such as Yokohama. Nevertheless, Wright was heartened by the fact that little structural damage had occurred to the hotel, and as electrical and water systems were still functioning, the hotel was being used as a centre for helping survivors. Mindful of Wright's interest in all things Japanese, it is strange that he never returned to Japan or to the hotel after its completion. Perhaps he had had enough.

Schindler, Neutra, Mendelsohn and Buckminster Fuller

Wright's Wasmuth publications and later the success of the Imperial Hotel attracted great interest in the United States and abroad. Many pondered the new ideas and a few managed to realize them, among them two young architects from Vienna. Rudolph Schindler arrived in Chicago and eventually worked for a short time with Wright in his Oak Park studio and later in Los Angeles on the design and construction supervision of several buildings, including Aline Barnsdall's Hollyhock House; but he was aggressive and sought work on his own account, in some cases from Wright's own clients. The other architect, a friend of Schindler, Richard Neutra, was invited by Schindler to come to America and managed to secure a position for him with Wright. The success of the Imperial Hotel later inspired another, Erich Mendelsohn, a gifted young German architect to seek Wright out to ask his advice in 1924.

Another freethinker was Buckminster Fuller who had much in common with Wright, including difficulties in executing his best ideas. Fuller and Wright also liked to discuss and formulate ways that would make possible the design of a new type of tower first presented as **St. Mark's-in-the-Bowerie** and later in its physical form as the Price Tower.

Out West

Most of Wright's other work was centred in the West, in the Los Angeles area and in Arizona, beginning in the late 1920s. He had been engaged by an earlier client for a new modest house in Pasadena. Alice Millard was married to George, a dealer in fine art and rare books in Chicago. They moved to Pasadena about 15 years later and George died there in about 1915. Alice took over her husband's business and expanded it to include fine and rare antiques. She caught Wright's interest and he helped her find a lot that was charming but problematic as a building site. He devised a new construction system of large, square concrete blocks and agreed to take on part of the cost if it ran over budget. It did.

Wright moved, if only on a temporary basis, to Los Angeles, and shared his office with his son Lloyd who not only helped with the drafting but also with the construction supervision, and even became the contractor on at least one occasion. All the work in Los Angeles was residential and was based on the concrete block technique Wright used in the little Millard house.

Wright managed to secure a commission from the head of the National Life Insurance Company of Chicago. The site was a choice one, just north of the famed Chicago Water

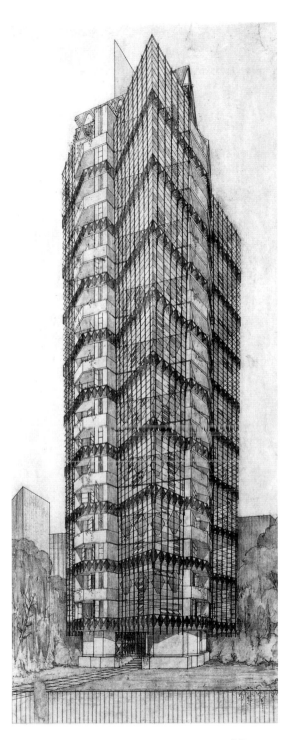

Tower. His client was Albert McArthur who had several brothers, one of whom bought Wright's Oak Park house and another became a playwright and lived for a short time in the apartment in the Oak Park studio. Eventually, Wright felt that his Los Angeles work was coming to an end and he could return to the Midwest. In November 1924, he announced that he was relocating his house and 12-position studio to 19 Cedar Street in Chicago, near the Charnley house he had designed while employed at Adler & Sullivan.

Wright was still suffering extreme aggravation from Miriam when he met a beautiful young woman, Olga Lazovitch Hinzenberg, a Montenegrin. She had recently arrived in the United States from Paris and had a young daughter, Svetlana, born in 1917. She was not quite divorced from her husband when she moved into Taliesin with Wright in February 1925. By November, a daughter Iovanna, Wright's seventh child, was born, but Miriam had been making such serious threats that Olgivanna had to leave the hospital prematurely with her three-day-old baby.

In Jail

These actions complicated Wright's life beyond any expectations. Wright was still married to Miriam Noel who was greatly angered by what had occurred and colluded

St. Mark's-in-the-Bowerie, New York City (1929)

There were to have been three of these identical towers for a very tight site in lower Manhattan where St. Mark's church remains. However, the design was later constructed for Harold Price in Oklahoma as the Price Tower of 1952

Miriam Noel Wright in 1919. Miriam was Wright's second wife after a long-delayed divorce from Catherine Tobin. Their marriage marked the beginning of a turbulent period in Wright's personal life

with Olga's husband, Vlademar Hinzenberg, to pursue the couple. A warrant was issued for the arrest of Wright for violating the Mann Act and a second suit for $250,000 followed, initiated by Hinzenberg for alienation. Wright and Olga had rented a cottage on Lake Minnetonka, not far from Francis Little's second house, so that he might have some peace and quiet while preparing his autobiography, which Olga had suggested he write. The two had rented the house under another name from the family of a judge who, it appears, discovered their real identities and turned them over to the Sheriff who was accompanied by a crowd when making the arrest. A news reporter was able to take a photograph while Wright was being ushered from the cottage and more scandal ensued.

Wright and Olgivanna spent a night in a Minneapolis jail and were again in the newspaper headlines. The story was carried for several days in the local and national press as Wright was also being held on an adultery warrant initiated by Hinzenberg, causing them to post bonds and attend various court appearances until the middle of November. At about this time, Miriam Noel made other assertions and attempted to take Taliesin away from Wright and for a time he was blocked from the property. Added to the disruption and expense of dealing with Miriam Noel, the bank also decided to make a claim for title to the property but Wright was fortunate in that he had a wonderful attorney in Phillip LaFollette who was able to straighten things out. However, Wright had to pay money over to Miriam Noel in order to finalize the divorce from her on 25 August 1927.

In Debt

Needless to say, there were few clients in these turbulent times and precious little income. Wright owed $43,000 to the Bank of Wisconsin and in July or September 1926 it impounded Taliesin to realize only $25,000 of it, leaving him still owing a balance. The bank was still holding Taliesin in May 1928 but by the following October, Wright's friends and clients had come to his aid and created Frank Lloyd Wright Incorporated in order to make responsible monetary decisions, take all his income, and distribute it wisely. The agreement was that Wright would work for the corporation, turning over all of his income, which in return would take care of Wright's debts, rescue Taliesin from the bank and provide a basic living for Wright and his immediate family, Olgivanna and the two children.

Wright married Olgivanna Lazovitch on 25 August 1928 at LaJolla in California, after which they visited the desert and enjoyed a honeymoon in Arizona before returning to Wisconsin.

In many architectural circles Wright was regarded as already dead or so old that his

Olgivanna Lazovitch, a beautiful Montenegrin and Frank Lloyd Wright's last wife

The Minneapolis jail where Frank Lloyd Wright and Olgivanna were imprisoned as a result of charges of alienation and adultery made by Miriam Noel Wright and Olgivanna's husband, Vlademar Hinzenberg

talents must be exhausted. This was not difficult to believe since he had only completed five buildings between 1925 and 1932. In addition, Wright had lost many opportunities to reinstate himself in the public eye and regenerate his architectural practice. Those he lost were not residential designs for anonymous clients but included the Doheny Ranch in Los Angeles in 1921, the National Life Insurance building in 1924, a three-apartment tower project for St. Mark's in New York, and the largest project of the 1920s, the Chandler resort and hotel in Arizona.

Arizona, Chandler and Ocotillo

Alexander Chandler had seen the tremendous potential of developing the land between the Midwest and California. In between was Arizona which had become a state in 1919 and was becoming famous for its healthy climate. Wright's introduction to Arizona and Chandler was a result of his being hired as a consultant by the son of an early Chicago client, Albert McArthur. McArthur had seen the Los Angeles concrete block work and thought that it could be used on the hotel he was designing for his two brothers just north of Phoenix – the Arizona Biltmore. The hotel was built and Chandler was inspired to contact Wright concerning a much larger

Ocotillo Camp, Nr. Chandler, Ariz. (1929)
This workspace for Wright and his draftsmen was located near to the site of the San-Marcos-in-the-Desert project for Alexander Chandler

The opening graphic for Book Four of Frank Lloyd Wright's autobiography

lacked. He trusted this architect to satisfy the needs and requirement of a modern manufacturing company, despite the fact that Wright was almost 70 years old.

Johnson's faith was amply rewarded when he received the drawings and the model of Wright's proposal, and he was enthusiastic to say the least. Moreover, he considered that he had received good value for his money – even though the job ran over the original budget – in the gratifying amount of publicity and interest generated by the design. Additions to the original building were made in the next decade that included an innovative research tower that served as a vertical counterpoint to the horizontal office block. Johnson was so pleased with the office building that he commissioned a house for himself, called Wingspread and, like Kaufmann, also commissioned additional work which, as was also the case with Kaufmann, remained unbuilt.

Taleisin West

Wright had enjoyed good health all his life, despite the fact that he was approaching the age of 70. However, in 1936 he contracted pneumonia and was hospitalized and his doctor considered it no longer wise for him to spend winters in cold, damp Wisconsin. Wright's reply was to purchase 800 acres (320 hectares) in the desert north-east of Phoenix

in Scottsdale, with the idea of transferring his entire architectural practice as well as his school operations there each winter. It was called Taleisin West. The construction of it was another experiment to be carried out by his staff and students but in the process Wright recovered and with what seemed like renewed energy attacked what would be the busiest period of his long career.

A House for Everyman

Wright's earlier career had been devoted to mainly residential work and this trend continued into his second. At the time of the design of Fallingwater and the Johnson Wax building, Wright had designed two very

similar houses, one of which was in Madison for a newspaper man, Herbert Jacobs and his family. Jacobs challenged Wright in 1936 to produce a design which could be built for $5,000 to which Wright responded by producing a brilliant solution that involved wooden walls without studs and a concrete floor without a basement. Heating was to be supplied by a boiler servicing pipes running under the concrete mat. To keep costs low, Wright specified the same brick that was being used for Johnson Wax and from time to time he would instruct his apprentices to take a car-load of culled bricks over to the Jacobs house, some of which were more than serviceable. The house – **Jacobs I** –

LEFT and OVERLEAF
**The Paul R. Hanna House
(The Honeycomb House),
Palo Alto, Calif. (1937)**

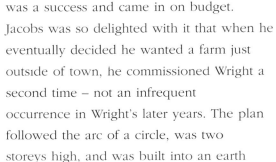

was a success and came in on budget. Jacobs was so delighted with it that when he eventually decided he wanted a farm just outside of town, he commissioned Wright a second time – not an infrequent occurrence in Wright's later years. The plan followed the arc of a circle, was two storeys high, and was built into an earth bank. The building was produced extremely economically due to the fact that the labour was largely supplied by the client and his wife.

Hearing of the economy of the first Jacobs house, Loren Pope, from an area of Washington, D.C., and himself also a newspaperman, contacted Wright for details of the Jacobs house with a view to building it for himself. With a few alterations because of the slope of the site, Pope got his house but for a little more than the Jacobs original. However, Pope got on well with Wright and was more than pleased with the result, which led him to write an article on the experience for *House Beautiful*.

The Edgar Kaufmann House (Fallingwater), Mill Run, Penn. (1936)

FAR LEFT
The Edgar Kaufmann House (Fallingwater), Mill Run, Penn. (1936)

LEFT
Taliesen West, Scottsdale, Ariz. (1938)
The former signpost at the entrance to Taliesin West

While the magazine was a popular one, no one quite expected the amount of favourable public reaction it generated. In fact, no fewer than 30 new clients came forward after reading Pope's account and Wright was mightily impressed with the power of publicity and could see nothing wrong in seeking a little more.

More Publicity

Wright developed a good working relationship with Elizabeth Gordon, the editor of *House Beautiful*. She had already written an article that had been highly critical of Le Corbusier and other exponents of the 'International Style', to which Wright responded. He offered her his services, the nature of which she at first failed to understand, but the outcome was that Wright placed two members of his own staff on the magazine for many years. There followed a string of articles on Wright's own work and on the work of architects and designers close to him which popularized Wright to such an extent that commissions were increased.

Everybody Loves Frank

Wright's staff were so well trained in his ways that they were able to increase the quantity of designs without their quality suffering. Wright had no need to search out clients as other architects did, through contacts, but could rely on his celebrity status to attract clients to his practice. It became quite the thing to have a Wright design, as is the case today, though this does not imply that this second wave of clients were being swept along on a tide of fashion or that they were not interested in good design or in Wright's ideas on the subject.

The climate of culture that developed within the Fellowship at Taliesin and Taliesin West was a rich one. The apprentices were expected to develop Wright's designs, supervise their construction, cook and clean the premises as well as farm the land and build and maintain the buildings. Several of the staff developed into proficient farmers, cooks and contractors besides being good architects. All work was meant to have a purpose and be executed with a certain flair and integrity that would reflect the overall philosophy of the Fellowship.

At the evening meal, men were expected to wear a coat or jacket, with dresses for the women, while on Saturday nights, dinner was more formal with tuxedoes and evening gowns in evidence. As well as the meal itself being more elaborate, special guests would

ABOVE
Frank Lloyd Wright's funeral cortège in 1959

RIGHT
An extract from *House Beautiful*, a book written by William C. Gannet which was printed by Wright and William Winslow on Winslow's hand letterpress

also be invited which included such luminaries as Pablo Cassals, Senator Adlai Stevenson, Alexander Woolcott, Paul Robeson, Mies van der Rohe, Ann Baxter and Michael Todd. After dinner, entertainments would take the form of a programme of music, a dance routine, or a film, examples of all forms and periods being represented over the years. Many of the apprentices became proficient musical intrumentalists or dance choreographers as well as talented exponents of other art forms – it certainly made for a rich life to be part of this group.

Death of a Legend

Even by the time of Wright's 90th birthday there seemed to be little diminution in his powers and his work was as vigorous as ever. At 88 he had designed the Guggenheim Museum for New York's Fifth Avenue. He was also working on an opera house and a

university for Baghdad as well as churches, synagogues and handfuls of houses. But his largest project, the Marin County Civic Center, to be built just across San Francisco's Golden Gate Bridge, was to be his last big project.

Wright was one of the most celebrated men of his age, even appearing on television when he was interviewed by Hugh Downs and Mike Wallace. He had written several more books on his own work and the philosophy of architecture and had lectured and was granted titles and awards from many countries and universities. His nation's architectural organization, which he had so far avoided joining, had awarded him their highest honour in the form of the AIA Gold Medal at their largest gathering in 1949.

Wright's clients adored him and, contrary to popular belief, not one of them considered him arrogant because, since it is the client that engages the architect, it is his job to please them and he did just that. He was an excellent salesman and could usually manage to inspire them with his own ideas, though he was willing to listen to clients' wishes and, if he was able, carry them out. This is one of the reasons why there is such a rich diversity in his work. His clients were all individuals and he was eager for them to realize their own desires.

The Fellowship was in residence in Arizona when Wright fell ill on 9 April 1959 and died quietly and unexpectedly of a coronary thrombosis. He was buried in the family cemetery in the Jones Valley after a short, well attended memorial service.

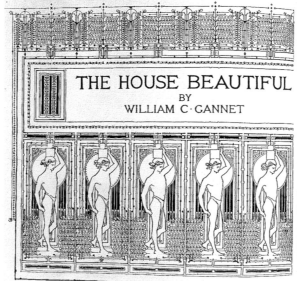

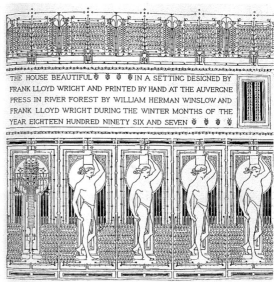

This photograph of Frank Lloyd Wright appeared on the cover of *Time* magazine in 1938, the beginning of Wright's golden age

CHAPTER TWO
Early Houses 1887–1910

Frank Lloyd Wright lost no time practising his calling once the idea of becoming an architect occurred to him. In 1887, while employed by Joseph Lyman Silsbee, an exponent of what is known as the Shingle Style, his aunts Nell and Jane decided to exploit his budding talents and their brother Thomas' construction abilities and have the 20-year-old Frank design for them his first building. This was the first Hillside Home in Spring Green in which they sited their new boarding school, and took the form of an oversized house covered with wooden shingles, no doubt influenced by Silsbee, and with several gables. It stood at the south end of the Jones Valley until Wright himself, after the founding of the Taliesin Fellowship in the 1930s, demolished it.

Wright was married early in June 1889 and designed a house for himself and his new bride, Catherine Tobin. Being a progressive architect, the house was wired for electricity before his Oak Park neighbourhood received the service. This too was covered with wooden shingles but the geometry of the

Frank Lloyd Wright's Own House and Studio, Oak Park, Ill. (1889–1909)

OPPOSITE
The west elevation of the 1889 house

LEFT
The entry to the studio

OVERLEAF
The interior of the 1895 playroom addition to the 1889 house

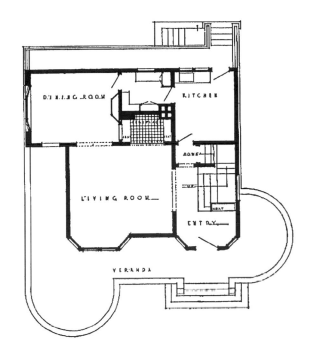

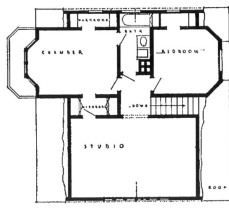

storey-and-a-half playroom. The interior walls were of brick and the ceiling was arched with a large skylight.

The success of the 1895 addition and a windfall of cash may have coincided and prompted Wright to add another building onto the house, his architectural studio, where he could pursue his own work and develop his innovative ideas. This building focused on the busy main street, Chicago Avenue, leaving the house itself fronting the residential street. The Studio certainly embodies the idea of form following function as each function had its own, clearly defined form with drafting room, offices and a library/conference room. The building was covered in wooden shingles that matched the adjacent house and the fence that ran along Chicago Avenue was itself also covered in shingles.

A series of modest houses in much the same style followed Wright's own house, two of them built on a speculative basis for a neighbour, **Walter Gale**, and two for individual clients, **Robert G. Emmond** and **Francis Woolly**, the first two being the opposite way round to the last. There are small differences in the roof profiles but the plans are nearly identical and the houses appear small but are actually quite roomy while the walls of the bays more than half consist

design was much simplified over his earlier building and of many others of the period and was the forerunner of what would come to be known as the Prairie style over the next few decades. The living room fireplace had a Romanesque arch and a central position which Wright felt to be important in defining the centre of the household and which he continued in his later houses, as well as certain other decorative features which included large flower urns positioned near or at house entrances. Wright did not dispense with all the historical devices but positioned the traditional Palladian window in a prominent location on the main façade. The interior rooms

were defined by screens rather than separated by doors and their colours were soft and brightened at the chair rail halfway up the walls.

Wright had probably never considered how large his family would eventually become and over a period of ten years consequently needed to make some adjustments to accommodate them. Taking the studio behind the Palladian window and adding a 6ft (1.8m) high partition, it became two bedrooms. In 1895, he added onto the house on two sides, taking the original kitchen and making it into a dining room by adding a bay to the south. On the east, he extended the second floor, adding a large

of windows. Curiously, the side elevations in all cases are symmetrical but other buildings are built too close to the Wright designs for them to be seen clearly. The fireplaces at the centre of the houses allow them to service two rooms, the parlour and the dining room. **Robert P. Parker**, an attorney, bought his house from Gale early in the process and his name appears on the working drawings.

In the neighbourhood of Kenwood, two friends bought their building lots on the same day from the same source and hired the same young architect and Wright designed two very different houses simultaneously. The **Blossom** and **McArthur Houses** remain on a short street on Chicago's south side, the McArthur house being similar to those of the Gale and Emmond houses with corner bays on one side. Rather than a front door facing the street, the door is at the side, up the driveway. It has a gambrel or hipped roof with Dutch Colonial influences.

The Blossom house is a departure from Wright's early work in that it is full-blown Colonial Revival, the design having a semi-circular front porch with Ionic columns and symmetrical façades on three sides. The Roman brick extends the foundation and the wood-

OPPOSITE

The Walter Gale House, Oak Park, Ill. (1893)

LEFT

The Robert G. Emmond House, La Grange, Ill. (1892)

The Francis J. Woolley House, Oak Park, Ill. (1893)

framed building sits upon it. The Blossom plan follows what Wright began in his own 1889 Oak Park house. The three bands are subdivided and the dining room circular bay softens and extends the square. The interior also shows some advance in his thinking. The large baseboard, simple walls and large room openings are all simplifications of the popular Victorian style.

Wright is credited with several designs while employed with Joseph Lyman Silsbee and Adler & Sullivan, though these cannot be properly substantiated.

The independent work of Wright after he left Adler & Sullivan begins with the **William Winslow House** of River Forest in 1893, the design being another departure from his earlier work and is unique in the Wright oeuvre. The house is severely symmetrical at its front, being

The Robert P. Parker
House, Oak Park, Ill.
(1892)

modern era rather than from over 100 years ago.

Robert W. Roloson was the son-in-law of Edward C. Waller of River Forest. He was in real estate and hired Wright in 1894 to design for him four city row houses, these being Wright's only designs in this style. There is ornamentation on the balusters of the front fence as well as spandrel panels between the windows and the interior stairway runs around a skylight which illuminates the otherwise sombre area; there is an adjacent interior court that also lends light to the dining room, the library and the inner hall.

Wright had adapted a popular historical style in the Blossom house of three years earlier and when his Forest Avenue neighbour, attorney **Nathan G. Moore**, requested a half-timbered house, he was experimenting with familiar styles and detailing. The house itself is symmetrical on the north and south façades with a large American porch on the garden or south side, while the interior centre third of the house is the stairway and a central hall. The property is actually three narrow lots, two of which are vacant, the third, at the sidewalk, being where the house is located.

On Christmas night, 1922, there was a fire which consumed the roof and the second floor but spared most of the first

OPPOSITE
The George Blossom House, Chicago, Ill. (1892)

LEFT
The Warren McArthur House, Chicago Ill. (1892)

as simple as his own house of four years earlier though more horizontal in form. The house has a band of beautiful, iron-spot Roman brick extending from the limestone base to the second floor window sill. Above this is a wide band of decorative plaster, reminiscent of Sullivan. The low pitched roof was once covered with orange clay tiles that nearly matched the brick as well as the plaster frieze. Today, one would be forgiven for mistaking the design for a product of the

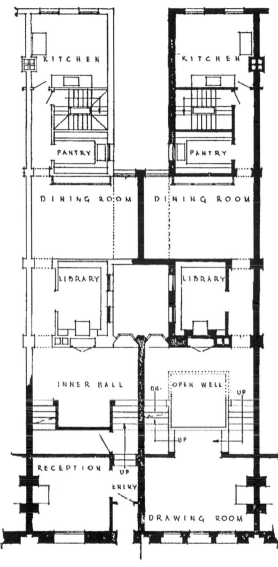

OPPOSITE
The William H. Winslow House, River Forest, Ill. (1893)

LEFT
The Robert W. Roloson Row Houses, Chicago, Ill. (1894)

floor. Wright was asked to design alterations and reconstruct the missing parts of the 1895 house and what he concocted is what is seen today. It is an amalgamation of the original Tudor style with Roman brick and terra cotta accents surmounted by Sullivanesque ornamentation. Charles E. White assisted in the construction supervision being the son-in-law of Charles E. Roberts; he had previously worked in Wright's studio before he opened his own practice.

Chauncey L. Williams inherited $100,000 from his father while a student at the University of Wisconsin at Madison and decided to become a publisher in 1895. He moved to River Forest, near to William Winslow, and commissioned a large house. The Wallers, Winslows, Williams and Wrights shared many social occasions and Williams asked Wright to

make some alterations to the house in about 1901 when the dormers were upgraded and a few windows removed. There is said to be an Orlando Giannini mural, now sadly overpainted. The same artist also produced a poster for a company in which Williams had an interest, namely the Turner Brass Works.

Harrison P. Young had a modest house in Oak Park, originally built for him by William E. Coman in 1870 but which was remodelled by Wright in 1895. Its steeply pitched roof makes it untypical of other Wright houses in the neighbourhood, though it is characteristic of Wright's work of the 1890s.

The roof dormer was added after Wright's work was finished but otherwise the **Harry C. Goodrich House** of 1896 is mostly original. The base of the house follows up over the window on the south side façade, which was a common Wrightian device. The gable emerging through the hipped roof was also used more than once, as in the Freeman house of Hinsdale.

A successful businessman, **Charles E. Roberts**, was another in a small circle of patrons. He commissioned some alterations to his own house and stable and also requested designs for several large housing blocks and subdivisions. It was Roberts who put forth Wright's name

on the building committee of the Unitarian Church after the wooden structure had burned down.

Warren Furbeck was a successful Oak Park stockbroker who commissioned Wright to provide the design for a new house as a wedding present for his son George in 1897 and another for his son Rollin six months later. The two houses are very different, as one would expect, being designed for two different clients. The **George Furbeck House** is symmetrical from the front with two

unusual towers, one containing the stairway, the other part of a room having no particular function. Several of the rooms are octagonal but are not expressed as such on the exterior. The original front porch had a simple roof above and low brick walls below. It was enclosed in 1922. The dormer was a similar addition after Wright's work had been completed. George and his new wife lived in the house for only two years.

Except for the porch on the right, the

OPPOSITE and LEFT
The Nathan G. Moore House, Oak Park, Ill. (1895)
On Christmas night 1922, a fire broke out and the second floor of the original house was destroyed, which was an opportunity for Wright to improve on the design, which he did

Like its predecessor, the Warren McArthur house of 1892, the **Isidor Heller House** has a left side entrance. This allows the room at the front to be more spacious rather than split by a corridor or cramped by a side hall. It also keeps useless walkways to a minimum. In the case of the Heller house, the stairway has a central location. This is one of the tallest of Wright's early houses, a full three storeys. Around the third storey is a detailed plaster frieze modelled by Richard Bock which features a Sullivanesque floral pattern with female figures, hands joined, at its centre. It is unfortunate that in attempts to restore the house in the 1970s, the delicate plaster was sandblasted with the result that much of its detail was lost. It has since been protected and it is hoped that the current owner will allow more access to the restoration than has earlier been the case. Another feature which has not been seen until recently was the tapestry brick, the horizontal bands of alternating colours adding a subtle touch to the otherwise vertical composition.

The most striking feature of the **George W. Smith House** is the angled break in the roofline, although the detailing of the house would be more appropriate on a stucco house than one with wooden shingles. There are no

OPPOSITE
The Chauncey L. Williams House, River Forest, Ill. (1895)

LEFT
The Harrison P. Young House, Oak Park, Ill. (1895)

Rollin Furbeck House is symmetrical and appears narrow from the front but is in fact very deep. The most striking feature is the large plate-glass window in the centre of the composition, being so large that it appears out of proportion. Because of its size, it would also seem to be a later addition as it was not in evidence in the June 1900 *Architectural Record* article by Robert Spencer. Rollin lived in his wedding present for only one year and his next house was designed for him by Wright's associate during his Silsbee years, George Washington Maher.

OPPOSITE
The Harry C. Goodrich House, Oak Park, Ill. (1896)

LEFT
The Charles E. Roberts House, Oak Park, Ill. (1896)

The George Furbeck House, Oak Park, Ill. (1897)

photographs to determine its earlier appearance. The wall and pier trim follows around corners defining a folded plane as would be seen ten years later on the interior of Unity Temple. Smith was a salesman for the prestigious Marshall Field & Company of downtown Chicago.

William Adams was a contractor and built the Emmond and Goan houses

before getting his own Wright design in 1900. Wright maintained he did not like double-hung windows which in this case appear to be at the client's request. Casement windows were Wright's preference and may have been costlier.

The building that signifies the beginning of the first great period of Wright's career is the **B. Harley Bradley House**. Its importance is apparent in the

simplicity of the stucco walls and the windows gathered, organized and tied together by bands of wood trim. Wright removed all ornament from trim and surfaces, leaving it on the windows that were characterized by a severe geometry. With its wonderful site on the north shore of the Kankakee river, one wonders why it was not oriented towards it rather than the street. The

The Rollin Furbeck House, Oak Park, Ill. (1897)

RIGHT and BELOW

**The Isidor Heller House,
Chicago, Ill. (1896)**

Bradley house was the first to incorporate Wright's simplified oak furniture. Wright had used the tall-backed chairs five years previously but they are not as pure as those of the Bradley house.

Next door is the **Warren Hickox House** designed at about the same time as the Bradley house, Mrs. Bradley being Warren Hickox's sister, Anna M. Hickox. The Hickox is perhaps of an even more advanced design than the Bradley and, without being overtly so, has a definite Japanese feel to it. The floor plan is remarkable because of the precedent it sets; the three-part living area consisting of library, living and dining rooms is part of a larger space that is subdivided only by indications of walls and decks that hang below the pitched ceiling. This three-part arrangement was used in several other houses over a ten-year period, the low decks serving not only as visual indicators but also often containing structural steel members that held the outside walls in position. There was a full suite of furniture designed for the

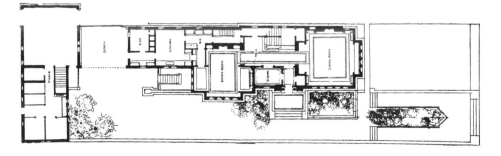

house but no early interior photographs appear to exist.

In contrast to the subtle Japanese influences of previous designs, the **Stephen A. Foster House**, designed in 1900, makes the Japanese element even more apparent. The upturned ends of the roofs along the gable, the dormers as well as the entry gateway and even the detailing on the garage are purposefully Japanese. Foster was a judge and may have used the house as a vacation retreat, it being so far out of the centre of the city's population at the time of its construction. As in the Goodrich and the Freeman house of Hinsdale, the gable through hip roof continues to be used.

E.H. Pitkin was one of Wright's Oak Park neighbours who, knowing that Wright had already designed houses around Lake Michigan, requested him to design for him a vacation lake house. This house was accessible only by boat and was only likely to be used for about

ABOVE LEFT
The George W. Smith House, Oak Park, Ill. (1896)

ABOVE
The William Adams House, Chicago, Ill. (1900)

two months in every year because of the cold and snow that did not fully melt until late May, only to return again in September or certainly by October and ensuring that the water would never warm up. Sapper Island, Desbarats, Ontario, is at the top of Lake Huron, just east of Sault Ste. Marie and the area would have been serviced by both train and lake ferries. The island is quite small and very rocky and the house faces west to catch as much sun as possible.

In keeping with Wright's interest in Japanese design, the **E. Arthur Davenport House** of 1901 continues to use familiar elements such as the upturned gable ends and flared base. This is one of the few known to have been designed in a rare partnership with H. Webster Tomlinson, his association with Wright lasting less than three years. There once was a porch, its low wall extending from the square bay at the front.

There was a large contingency of Chicago area residents who, independently, sought their own vacation and weekend house sites along the south shore of Lake Delavan, Wisconsin, the **Henry Wallis House** being the earliest of these built in 1900. Wallis never inhabited or used the building but sold it soon after its completion to Dr. H. Goodsmith. In many ways it is similar to the south Chicago Adams house of about the same date. Wright also designed a yacht club that was demolished long ago and which was located at the far east end of South Shore Drive.

The largest Wright-designed house on

OPPOSITE and ABOVE
The B. Harley Bradley House, Kankakee, Ill. (1900)

RIGHT and OPPOSITE BELOW
**The E. Arthur Davenport
House, River Forest, Ill.
(1901)**
The smaller picture shows the
original configuration of the
house which was later
remodelled

LEFT

E.H. Pitkin House, Sapper Island, Ontario, Canada (1900)

The **Charles S. Ross House** was once sheathed in horizontal wooden battens. The simple, plain surfaces and the handling of the volumes give it a more modern appearance than its 1902 date would indicate.

One of the smallest lots on the south shore contains the **George W. Spencer House** and the north prow is in keeping with the nautical feeling of its lakeside setting.

One imagines the most perfect

Prairie house having long, low-pitched overhanging roofs, ribbon windows, massive piers and extensions onto the gardens. The **A.P. Johnson House** of 1905 fulfills all of these requirements though it has been little publicized and is therefore little known. The building itself has been resurfaced and the interior remodelled to such a point that one can hardly identify it as a Wright design at all.

If one were to take the earlier

**The Henry Wallis House,
Delavan, Wisc. (1900)**

**The Fred B. Jones House,
Delavan, Wisc. (1900)**

LEFT and BELOW
**The Charles S. Ross House,
Delavan, Wisc. (1902)**

Hickox house and make the gables into hipped roofs and move the entry porch 90° to the side, one would have the **F. B. Henderson House** of Elmhurst. It was built about a year after the Hickox but in so many ways is identical to it. In this form it appears less inviting than with the open gables.

As any father would, James C. Rodgers wanted the best for his daughter. When she married **Frank W. Thomas,** Rodgers asked Wright to design their house and it is located at the south end of Wright's own Forest Avenue

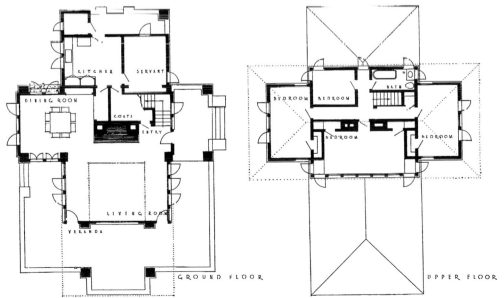

The George W. Spencer House, Delavan, Wisc. (1902)

in Oak Park. By Wright's own definition, this is the first of the Prairie houses. The main rooms are up off the ground, there is no basement and the windows, which are spectacular, are gathered into groups. The tall walls extend to the sidewalk and are intended to be inviting but are in fact slightly intimidating; however, as one passes below the arch and up the stairs the effect is somewhat modified. The house was resurfaced by Robert Coleman and remains one of the few Wright houses on Forest Avenue in Oak Park still in its original colours.

One has a vision of a Wright-designed Prairie house as being low and horizontal, hugging the ground. Wright was never one to adhere to the rules,

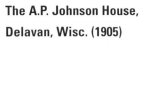

The A.P. Johnson House,
Delavan, Wisc. (1905)

RIGHT and BELOW
The F.B. Henderson House, Elmhurst, Ill. (1901)

OPPOSITE, LEFT and RIGHT
The Frank W. Thomas House, Oak Park, Ill. (1901)

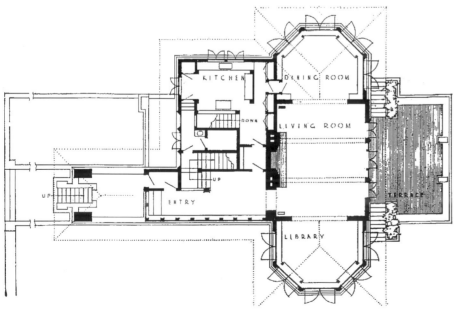

even if he made them himself. The **William G. Fricke House** of 1901 is certainly a full three storeys tall and yet retains all of the other characteristics of a Prairie design.

A father and son built summer houses adjacent to one another in Whitehall, Michigan, which is at the east end of a lake that feeds into Lake Michigan and provides a safe harbour. **George E. Gerts** and his son, Walter, were River Forest neighbours of Wright who did a little remodelling job on Gerts' River Forest house several years later.

Both of these buildings have now been altered almost to the point of being unrecognizable as Wright's work.

Arthur Heurtley was a banker at the prestigious Northern Trust Company in Chicago and his house certainly gives an impression of wealth and security, the canted brick walls adding to its feeling of solidity. The brick prow that defines the front porch clearly indicates the front entrance without being an invitation to enter. The Heurtley house is the second one in two blocks of Forest Avenue, both on the east side of the street, to have arched entryways, the Frank Thomas being the other. Like the Thomas house, the Heurtley also has its main rooms on the second level with no damp basement. Rather than expanding into the landscape, the building is compact except for the wall that extends to the south. The dining room is on the left and the living room is in the central part of the house with a porch to the south side. Inside the massive hipped roof are large wooden trusses that allow the rooms below to be so open and there is a window in the back of the chimney that lights the attic. In the living room are two large ceiling panels with art glass behind which have electric light bulbs providing illumination. They are not skylights. The pitched dining room ceiling is lit with what might be the first

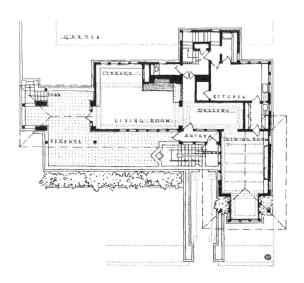

form of cove lighting to be introduced into Wright's work.

At the same time, Heurtley had Wright prepare a design for a remodelling of a summer home on a small island in northern Michigan. It is an island owned by a private club which counted such wealthy people as Henry Ford among its members. The site of the summer house is one of the best on the island with a view to the south and west.

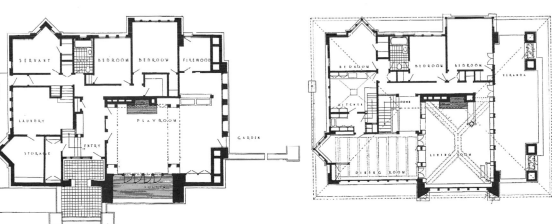

OPPOSITE and THIS PAGE
**The Arthur Heurtley House,
Oak Park, Ill. (1902)**

LEFT
**The Heurtley Cottage on
Marquette Island, Mich.
(1902)**

RIGHT and OPPOSITE
The Ward W. Willits House,
Highland Park, Ill. (1901)

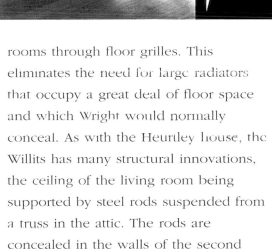

There are no roads on the island making it accessible only by boat; the season is only about six weeks long because of the very cold winters in this part of Michigan.

The first house of Wright's design that could be termed a masterpiece is the **Ward W. Willits House** of 1901. It is located on a large site facing south-west and populated with tall oak trees. This house does have a basement and it contains large air ducts with heat pipes inside. The ducts take in fresh outside air and heats it before it flows into the rooms through floor grilles. This eliminates the need for large radiators that occupy a great deal of floor space and which Wright would normally conceal. As with the Heurtley house, the Willits has many structural innovations, the ceiling of the living room being supported by steel rods suspended from a truss in the attic. The rods are concealed in the walls of the second floor bedroom.

At first sight, the side wings appear to be collinear but are on offset axes making the first floor plan a pinwheel.

Wright repeated this idea in Wingspread, the Johnson house, almost 40 years later.

The rooms are large, the living room being about 24 x 27ft (7.3 x 8.2m). There are few walls separating the first floor rooms, which produces the feeling of space flowing between them. The partitions are short, their top halves forming spindle oak screens. Often, the bottom halves are bookcases.

The dining room is perhaps the most interesting space: it has extensions out to the end with a very large open porch and to the left side, a smoking porch.

**The Susan Lawrence Dana
House, Springfield, Ill,
(1903)**

The ceiling has skylights through which the sun pours and there are ceiling lights fitted with electric light bulbs. Below each are laylights with art-glass patterns interdigitating with one another to produce a quadraline form. The breakfront is both built-in (the bottom) and free-standing (the top glass cabinets), another Wright hybrid.

When the **Susan Lawrence Dana House**, Springfield, Illinois was published in the 1910 Wasmuth portfolio, Wright dated the design 1899. It could not have been an error as it was completed less than seven years earlier. One proposal is that Wright felt it should be placed back in another century rather than in 1903, just four years later.

This building contains many of the finest examples of Wright's genius in several categories. The art glass is unsurpassed in both quality of design as well as execution. The furniture includes some unique pieces, one that combines the woodwork and art glass in a free-standing piece as well as the famous print table. While not the first of Wright's buildings to integrate sculpture, the

The Susan Lawrence Dana House, Springfield, Ill, (1903)

entry piece, 'Flower in the Crannied Wall' is the best.

The building takes up nearly the entire lot, if one includes the remodelled barn, now a coachhouse. What is now seen as the Dana house incorporates an earlier Victorian farmhouse owned by her father for many years and left to Susan Dana upon his death. She hired Wright to design the building that now surrounds it. There is one room that was kept in nearly original condition and which is known as the Victorian Room.

Two of the rooms, the dining room

and the gallery, are smaller scaled adaptations of the main dining room from Adler & Sullivan's Auditorium Building as well as being based on the playroom from Wright's own Oak Park house. Each of these examples had a barrel vault. The feature that Wright adds to what might otherwise be an uninspired room is a relieving element at each end. In the gallery, Wright allows for a semi-circular plate-glass window in front of which and from a wooden frame are suspended nine panels of art glass. They are hung as if they were tapestries.

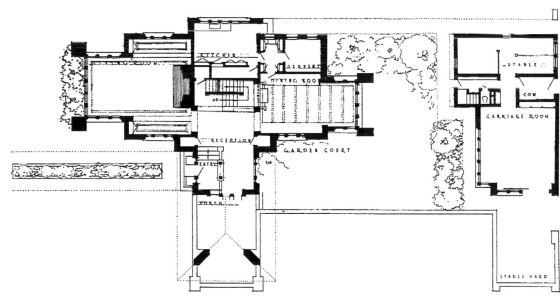

The Francis W. Little House, Peoria, Ill. (1903)

95

This is the only example of the hanging system in all of Wright's work.

The furniture completes what Wright began with the architecture. While there are many built-ins, they are mostly cabinets or bookcases. There is no integral seating, rare in a Wright design of any era. The reason for this might be that it was a house for entertaining. Since

the events could take any form, the house and the location of the furnishings would have needed to be as adaptable as possible and free-standing furniture was the practical solution, Wright being more than equal to the task.

Susan Dana outlasted all of her family, including her children, parents and three husbands. While far from

destitute, she lived her last years in a small building next door to the magnificent house her father had built and that she had so greatly transformed. However, the house had not been maintained properly and she later abandoned it.

The drawings for the **Francis W. Little House** in Peoria, built in 1903,

OPPOSITE LEFT
The Warren H. Freeman House, Hinsdale, Ill. (1903)

OPPOSITE RIGHT
The J.J. Walser House, Chicago, Ill. (1903)

LEFT
The William E. Martin House, Oak Park, Ill. (1903)

were noted with the same date as the Dana house and it was apparently completed first. The plan is similar to the Dana house, as is the arched front door, and the interior was as elaborate in many respects although the art glass was uninspired, leading one to think that Wright was concentrating all his efforts on the Dana house. Another Peoria client, Robert D. Clarke, bought this house a few years after it was built and had Wright design the alterations and additions. Little liked his house so much that he commissioned another one about ten years later.

The newly discovered **W.H. Freeman House** of Hinsdale seems to

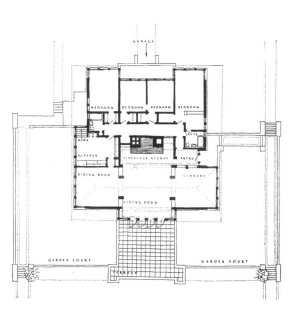

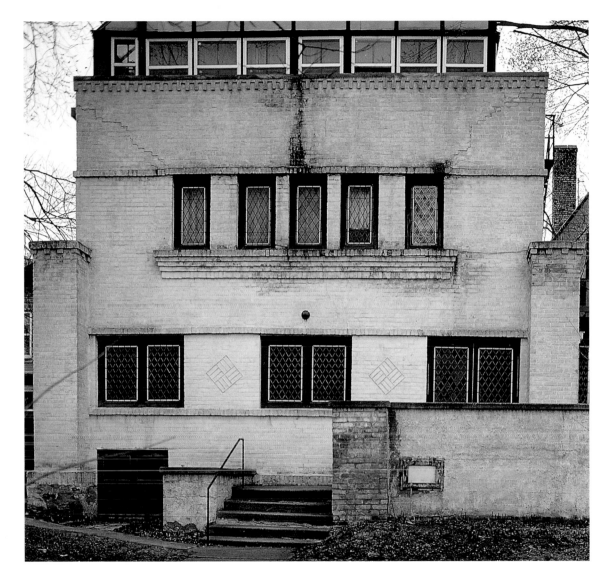

playroom. The best part of Martin's house is on the first floor and Wright handled the layout of the compact rooms in a masterful fashion. The entry hall brings one into the centre of the house and yet all the rooms can be seen without entering them, neither do they intrude on one another. The glass is a curiosity. It is the basis, the framework, for the fountain doors at the entry, reminiscent of the best glass of the Dana house; perhaps Martin had seen it and liked it.

The Martin house was on a large site. Originally, a wall extended south into the gardens defining the street from the private grounds. There is an indication of this wall having been rebuilt recently. A part of the property was sold off and another house was built on it.

The **J.J. Walser House** of 1903 is the first of a series of nearly identical designs. The house has the same kind of three-room arrangement as the Hickox and Henderson houses, the difference being that the three rooms run through the middle of the building and other rooms form wings on either side. Except for one Chicago house that is now gone, all of the examples have hipped roofs. As with all of Wright's buildings throughout his career, there were houses which were near copies rather than

OPPOSITE

The Edwin H. Cheney House, Oak Park, Ill. (1904)

LEFT

The Robert M. Lamp House, Madison, Wisc. (1904)

have disappeared from view because there is no record of Freeman ever having lived at this address, the house having being intended for rental. The building was constructed from Wright's design but Freeman decided to make some changes and the final result is slightly different from the drawings.

William E. Martin had heard about Wright's talents and asked for a house of his own to be built in Oak Park in about 1903. The result is a wonderful building: it is a three-storey house with a grand room at the top, scaled for children as a

identical because of the differences in the clients' objectives and preferences. The Walser house is a good solution.

Edwin H. Cheney was an electrical engineer and graduate of the University in Ann Arbor. He pursued his not-so-soon-to-be wife over several years and finally married her. Mamah Borthwick's family had moved to Oak Park and she was familiar with it when she and her new husband built their Wright design in 1904. The Cheney house utilizes the same three-part room scheme as the Hickox and the Henderson but with one important difference – it is all on one floor. The house is very low even for a one-storey structure, the height coming from the floor being at almost 6ft (1.81m) above the level of the front sidewalk. A deep porch on the front of the house had a medium-height brick wall which prevents foot and automobile traffic from looking into the house, and the bedrooms are along the back of the house off a corridor that is located behind the living room fireplace in the centre of the house. This hallway would be very dark except for a clever window that is installed in the back of the fireplace and is lit by an opening in the top of the chimney and which makes a tremendous difference to the hall. There was to be a garage built under the

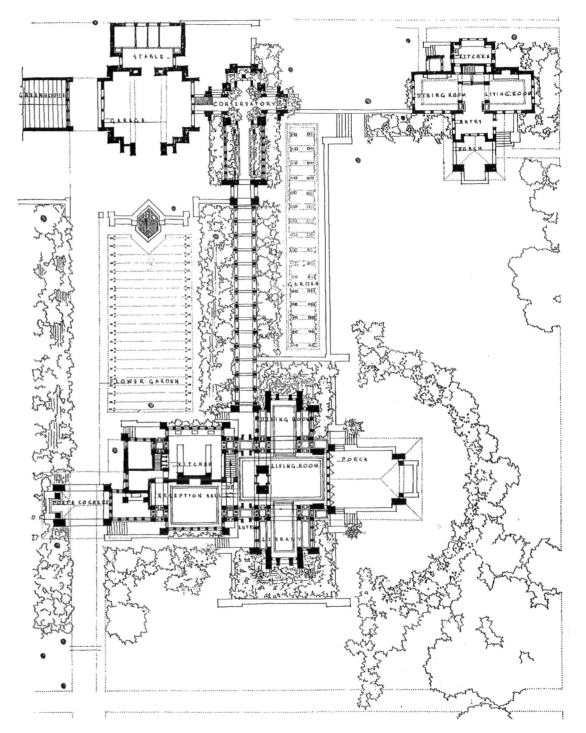

The Darwin D. Martin
House, Buffalo, New York
(1904)

The Darwin D. Martin House, Buffalo, New York (1904)

bedrooms but it is thought that the building commission would not allow it. Instead, the space was turned into a family and work space.

After Mamah and Wright's affair, Edwin Cheney and his new wife continued to live in the house until their move to St. Louis in 1926, more than ten years after Mamah's murder at Taliesin.

The Wrights and the Cheneys interconnected on a social and professional level, as evidenced by a social note in a Madison, Wisconsin newspaper that reported the two couples travelling by automobile to Madison to visit another Wright client, a long drive even by today's standards.

The client they visited was **Robert M.**

Lamp, a paraplegic who walked with crutches, and who had been a boyhood friend of Wright. The house was in the centre of a block near the State Capitol building and was in cubic form, quite unlike most of Wright's Prairie designs. One would have imagined that a house intended for someone who had difficulty walking might be on one level; however,

The Darwin D. Martin House, Buffalo, New York (1904)

The George Barton House, Buffalo, New York (1903)

the house is a three-storey building, up a steep incline and a long way from the street. The art-glass widow is embellished with a rather standard diamond pattern within a border.

George Barton was the brother-in-law of Darwin D. Martin, also of Buffalo and also an employee of the famous Larkin company. It was Darwin's brother, William, who was the first to employ Wright on a house design. Darwin Martin had purchased a large piece of property and the Barton house was located in one corner of it. The site plan must have been worked out long beforehand as it was well integrated once the other pieces were in place. The house for Barton was also a kind of experiment for Darwin Martin who was also interested in having Wright design a house for him, realized in 1904.

The Barton House was the first of Wright's Buffalo projects and he went on to complete six buildings in all, the one thread tying them all together being the Larkin company.

The Barton house was another in the line which contained the J.J. Walser house. It was in beautiful iron-spot Roman brick instead of stucco, and the detailing both inside and out was more refined. The art glass was iridescent and had Colonial-type cames or bars.

**The George Barton House,
Buffalo, New York (1903)**

Darwin Martin was general manager of the Larkin Company, a mail order company that once rivalled Sears & Roebuck and Montgomery Ward, both of Chicago. Martin was well paid and at one time was making $1,000,000 per annum at a time before income tax was initiated. Martin was a meticulous person who maintained daily diaries of his personal as well as professional life and kept copies of all the letters he wrote as well as those written to him; this is fortunate as these records are now housed at the University in Buffalo and are available for study.

Martin required a simple house and Wright gave it to him. Driving through the neighbourhood, one is struck with the relative size of the other mansions. They are built tall and are meant to indicate the social positions of their owners. **The Martin House** is large, but set well back from the street, the hipped roof adding to the feeling of tranquillity and making it appear shorter than a flat- or even a gable-roofed house. The house is composed of horizontals and has few vertical elements. Toward the inside of the site, and largely hidden from view, were a long pergola and a conservatory with attached stable and garage. To the side of the conservatory were greenhouses not easily discernible

from the street. The Martin house and its extensions were connected by a brick wall to the earlier Barton house and all buildings used the same materials and were scaled to complement one another.

The interior is one of the most complex of the Prairie era. In plan, it bears more of a resemblance to a plaid than a set of square rooms. There are several sets of four iron-spot Roman brick piers that hold bookcases with radiators at the centre of each pier set. The three-part room system was used on the east side of the house combining the library, the living room and the dining room in much the same manner as the earlier Hickox house with very complex and elaborate wood mouldings defining each of the spaces. A fine glass mosaic two way fireplace divides the living room from the entry and central hallway; the glass, however, is long since gone. A large reception room is situated opposite the living room from the hallway and the ceiling is treated with long strips of oak moulding placed laterally to the main axis. The floors were covered with speckled brown one-inch square ceramic tiles but to add warmth, a lime green wool carpet was placed over it, the green matching the colour of the glass in the windows and the heavily woven silk drapes. There is

very little wall surface and where it exists consists of plaster framed with more oak trim.

Some of the most refined furniture was designed for the Martin house, the pieces being unique to it and include a very comfortable round-backed chair of solid oak, a case for the new *Encyclopedia Britannica*, and a grandfather clock which complements the mouldings. Several tables provided surfaces for books, family games and cards. However, like the Dana house, there is no built-in furniture and there are three sets of couches, one of them incorporating a cabinet for books at the outside ends of the arms.

As with the Dana house, the glass is very fine but, unlike it, there is a single theme which is a central 'Tree of Life' motif which is repeated three times in the main windows. According to Martin's archive, he considered the heavy square base of the design too intrusive, complaining that it cut out his view. He wrote to Wright, providing him with his own sketches, and many of the first floor windows were altered.

The Martin house was abandoned for 15 years after Darwin's death in the early 1930s and many of the windows were removed, as was some of the furniture. The roof became leaky and caused the glass mosaic that surrounded the living room fireplace to deteriorate when it fell to the floor and was discarded. Thankfully, an active group has been formed which is doing a marvellous job of restoring the house to its earlier condition.

Little is known of **Mary M.W. Adams** and the history of her house in Highland Park, Illinois, built in 1905. She was very likely the oldest of all of Wright's clients and it is not known whether or not she was married, but she was very active in the Christian Science church in Highland Park though they have no information on her now. She died before she had lived in the house for two years.

It is a wonderful house, built with a view from the bluff above Lake Michigan and its clean stucco lines have not been altered. At the main corners are buttresses much like those of the rather larger Willits house on the other side of town, and the hipped roof contains the smaller elements of the lower two storeys.

Another enigmatic client is **Charles E. Brown** and a common name such as this has been difficult to trace. Brown did not live in Evanston and he may have been a patent attorney in Chicago. His intention was to have a group of Wright designs for which his house was

to be the model. This was the second property Brown owned, the other being futher to the west. It is a simplification of the *Ladies' Home Journal* Fireproof House design for $5,000. Instead of stucco, it is surfaced with horizontal wooden board and batten siding and the art-glass pattern is also a simple one. Thus far, there is no explanation for the extensions of the front façade. A stucco duplicate was built several years later in Indiana.

There are a few curved walls in Wright buildings and the **Hiram Baldwin House** in Kenilworth was one of them while the Dana, Winslow and Blossom houses are other examples. These latter had curved walls in the dining rooms but the Baldwin was the first to have them in the living room. The original art glass was very much like that for the William Martin house, being in the form of a thick grille or screen with repeating horizontal members.

Wright liked to imagine that these houses were out on the prairie, buried deep in swaying grasses; however, they would have stuck out like a sore thumb on such a flat landscape. Up to this date, 1905, virtually all of them were for flat city lots of limited size; however, the **William A. Glasner House** was built along the upper edge of a ravine in

The Mary M.W. Adams
House, Highland Park, Ill.
(1905)

**The Hiram Baldwin House,
Kenilworth, Ill. (1905)**

The Charles E. Brown
House, Evanston, Ill. (1905)

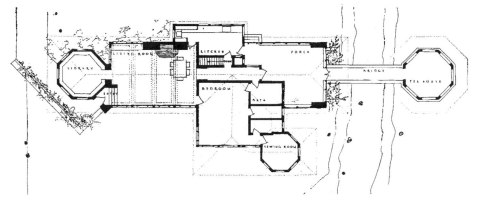

Glencoe, the ravine feeding the water out into Lake Michigan. The house assumes a horizontal floor line and the base follows the ups and downs of the ravine edge. There are two rooms that are octagonal, similar to those seen in the late 1890s in the Bagley and Furbeck houses and in the library of Wright's own studio. In the Glasner house, however, they are the library and a sewing room off a rear bedroom. There was to be a third room, accessed over an arched bridge to the tea room and was to have been aligned and opposite to the front library. There is a hope that it may be added to complete the original scheme. The living room has a pitched ceiling with heavy wood-trim boards. The windows are three-part units with a large, nearly square area of plate glass in the centre, flanked by two beautiful simplified Tree-of-Life patterns in soft iridescent colours. These sidelights are

OPPOSITE and ABOVE
The William A. Glasner House, Glencoe, Ill. (1905)

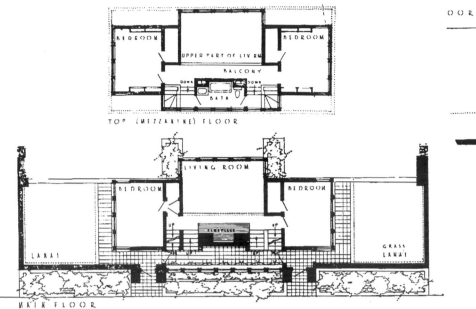

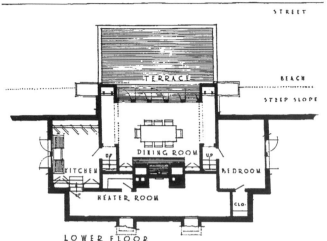

in the form of casement windows.

The **Thomas A. Hardy House** of Racine, also built in 1905, is unusual in that the design again takes its site into account and is all the better for it. From the street side, it appears to be another happy, compact Prairie design complete with hipped roof and gathered windows. On the side that faces Lake Michigan, it appears quite vertical and the interior is the first instance where Wright designed a two-storey space that is expressed on the exterior. The house is symmetrical and because it is located next to a park, is

The Thomas P. Hardy House, Racine, Wisc. (1905)

often mistaken for a public facility. It has a doorway at either end and one could easily assume that one entrance is for men and the other for women. The Hardy house is one of the newer and smaller houses on South Main Street in Racine.

William R. Heath was convinced by his brother-in-law, Elbert Hubbard, one of Larkin's best salesmen, that he should leave his Chicago law practice and join the Larkin Company in Buffalo. His Wright design was built in a more

prestigious neighbourhood than the cluster defined by the other three Buffalo houses and the Heath house is long and narrow and situated on a narrow lot, facing a street on the long side. Wright put the living room at the

The William R. Heath House, Buffalo, New York (1905)

The Peter A. Beachy House,
Oak Park, Ill. (1906)

end that faces the park and sited the dining room away from the street. Most but not all of the furniture was designed by Wright along with many built-ins. The glasswork was the first to combine more than two panels in the design, one more than the dining room lights of the Willits house. The red brick of the house is nearly identical to that used in the Larkin building and may have been from the same source. Heath

lived in his house almost until his death.

Like the Dana house, the **Peter A. Beachy House** of Oak Park also incorporates an earlier house to the point of obliterating it on the interior and the original Fargo house can only be seen at a few points in the basement. The lot is the largest residential property in Oak Park and the house does have seven gables, but there is no evidence that there was any attempt to relate it to the

The K.C. DeRhodes House, South Bend, Ind. (1906)

117

RIGHT
The P.D. Hoyt House, Geneva, Ill. (1906)

OPPOSITE
The George Madison Millard House, Highland Park, Ill. (1906)

type. The house is set well back from the street on several acres in what was originally a separate town when it was built. However, Batavia is now a Chicago suburb, one of the furthest west. The house has no art glass and is quite plain in other respects. Since no old interior photographs appear to exist, there is

nothing to suppose that Wright designed any furniture for the house.

A little way up the road from the Gridley house is the much smaller **P.D. Hoyt House** in Geneva. It is a modest building on a small city lot, its windows quite unadorned apart from a clear 'H' delineated by the muntin bars. The stucco

wall at the sidewalk was added much later by another owner and was not designed by Wright. Unlike most other Wright houses, the front door is located directly in the centre of the wall facing the street and there is no protection from the elements as the door opens directly into the living room.

**The George Madison
Millard House, Highland
Park, Ill. (1906)**

purchasing five acres initially, his holdings grew to over 600 acres (240 hectares), about a square mile of land. It has since been subdivided and sold off, and the Forest Preserve District now owns the land along the Fox river where the house is located. Wright's work was minor in proportion to the number of buildings that were erected for Fabyan. Wright remodelled an earlier house and expanded it, adding new roofs and rooms onto the original. Wright also designed the Fox River Country Club for the south portion of the Fabyan property. Those buildings have not survived.

LEFT
The Frederick D. Nicholas House, Flossmoor, Ill. (1906) Photograph taken after a remodelling which completely obscures Wright's original intentions

BELOW
The George Fabyan House, Geneva, Ill. (1907)

The Chicago literary scene revolved around **George Madison Millard** as he was a seller of fine and rare books at the famous A.C. McClurg's Wabash Avenue bookstore. He married a young girl from Evanston, Alice Parsons, and they were married in London in 1901, building their Wright house five years later. When the floor plan is studied it appears, as with the Robie house, that the main entry is from the back of the house. Visitors are not directed toward or past the living room until inside the house where it projects to the south lawn. The second-floor bedrooms have pitched ceilings. There once was a small built-in outdoor bench on the east side where the nearby Lake Michigan could be viewed.

Another four-square house was the **Fredrick Nicholas House** at Flossmoor, Illinois, on the south side of Chicago. However, in the last several years a major remodelling project has almost completely obscured Wright's original design.

One of the most fascinating of Wright's clients was **Colonel George Fabyan**, who was born in Boston and was the same age as Wright. His family had established a chair at the Harvard Medical College and were cotton textile merchants. When Fabyan arrived in Chicago in 1903 as a company representative, he already had interests in acoustics and horticulture. After

The Stephen M.B. Hunt House, La Grange, Ill. (1907)

A prime example of a Wright design was published in the April 1907 issue of *Ladies' Home Journal* and was realized in the **Stephen M.B. Hunt House** of La Grange. There is a departure from the published design in that the Hunt house is constructed on a wooden frame with a stucco surface. The solid corners contract with the centre of each elevation that is filled with windows. Of note, are the tall, thin fixed windows at each end of the main group. These slits frame and introduce the four-window group and without this important detail the windows are merely four holes in the wall. The offset position of the entry and stairway keep the forms pure and the rooms large. The trellis shown in the publication was never built onto the house. This design is one of the most economical ever devised. With one beam down the centre, the floors can be constructed from 2 x 12ft lengths with no cutting or trimming. At 32sq ft (3m²), a 16-ft (4.9-m) span is the maximum allowed by this size of pre-cut timber. The 34 windows are all the same size, adding another degree of economy. The wood trim on the exterior adds interest to the design but acts as a divider for large areas of stucco which is less likely to crack when there are subdivisions. The present appearance shows downspouts at each corner which

Wright would not have included.

The **Andrew Porter House** in the Jones Valley, Spring Green, Wisconsin is now part of the Taliesin complex and the Frank Lloyd Wright Foundation. Porter was married to Wright's sister and had previously bought the Heurtley House in Oak Park. He moved to Taliesin in 1907 and commissioned this house, assisting Wright in managing the estate in its early years. Porter brought the furniture up to this house when the Heurtley house was sold in the 1920s.

The Porter house is a near copy of the Hunt house but is sheathed in wooden shingles. The fenestration, however, is dramatically different from the Hunt and not as successful.

It is said that Elizabeth Sutton read about Wright's work and decided to hire him by mail and it is not known if Wright ever saw the **Harvey Sutton House** located in McCook, which is in south central Nebraska along a line of the Burlington Railroad. The Sutton house was one of the largest houses in McCook and was converted to medical offices for a time and has since been converted back to a residence. A water fountain has been built at the corner of the property.

Wright wrote about the **Ferdinand F. Tomek House** in Riverside, Illinois and

The Andrew T. Porter
House, Spring Green, Wisc.
(1907)

The Harvey P. Sutton House,
McCook, Neb. (1907)

**The Ferdinand F. Tomek
House, Riverside, Ill. (1907)**

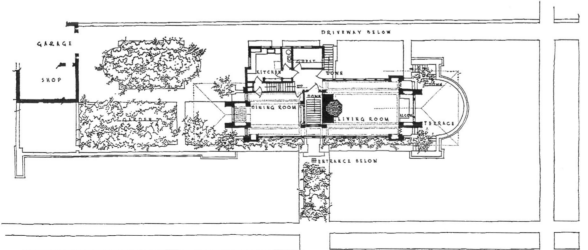

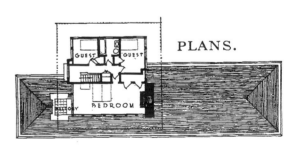

PLANS.

maintained that he used it as the model for his successful and famous Robie house. The Tomek was built in 1907 and has one of the few direct street entrances of the Prairie period. The house appears taller than the Robie for two reasons; first it *is* taller and second, the Robie house has a front yard that is dug out, further reducing the apparent height.

In Springfield, Ohio, the **Burton J. Westcott House** of 1907 has the familiar three-room arrangement but is rather different in concept. Rather than having a tall ceiling that connects through to all the rooms and with differentiation between the spaces using a continuous headband, the Westcott house has built-in bookcases with benches on the fireplace side. The side entrance was designed for the automobile, which was not widely used at the time; but Wright became a devotee and owned several sporty models, as did Westcott. This house also has the largest, most imposing vertical flower urns of all Wright's residential work. They stand over 6ft (1.8m) tall at the garden steps which makes them more imposing than if they were set back nearer to the building.

An associate of another of Wright's clients, Warren McArthur of Chicago, was **E.E. Boynton**. They were both representatives of the Ham Lamp company, the manufacturers of kerosene

lamps used by nearly all railroads and in many farmhouses and industrial operations before the widespread introduction of electricity. Boynton was a widow and his daughter assisted in the design. However, part of the property was sold off and lost its multi-level gardens and a tennis court. This design is much like the Heath house of Buffalo in its linear form and arrangement of the rooms. There is a full suite of furniture designed by Wright, most of it still in place. The furniture is owned by the local historical society and, if they wish, the owners are allowed to use it in the house for which it was intended, which is a

The Burton J. Wescott House, Springfield, Ohio (1907)

RIGHT and OPPOSITE
**The E.E. Boynton House,
Rochester, New York (1908)**

happy arrangement for both parties.

Wright's 1908 house for **Avery Coonley** at Riverside, Illinois was the largest residential project to be realized in Wright's prolific Prairie years. The site was on the extreme south-west end of Riverside, in a community laid out by landscape designer Frederick Law Olmsted in 1869. The site covered several acres and included in the Wright designs were a main house, stable, gardener's cottage and later a kindergarten (Coonley Playhouse). A former Wright employee, William Drummond, designed a residence for the kindergarten teachers. Wright developed several schemes for the location of the buildings and in most of these they appeared to be set on an axis. The site was surrounded on three sides by the Des Plaines river where a peninsula was created within a wide bend flowing from north to south, curving all the way round and ending in a northerly flow at the east end of the Coonley property. Wright's work on the project spanned the period before and after his affair with Mamah Borthwick Cheney.

Along with his brothers, Coonley was heavily involved in business as they owned a manufacturing company as well as a large cattle and sheep ranch in Texas. Avery Coonley was a director of *The Dial* magazine for which Wright had

designed an unexecuted plan of a building in downtown Chicago. He had no part in the Tabasco operation or involvement in the McIlhenny Company on Avery Island in Louisiana, as has been speculated, and both he and his brother, John Stuart Coonley, were Christian Scientists and active in church matters. The formalities of their religion had an effect on the location of certain elements in the main house. As a practitioner, Coonley was expected to interview other members of the church, one of the requirements being that a person going into an interview should not see another leaving; consequently, two separate stairways had to be utilized.

The main house was long with two wings projecting to the north, the living room facing south across a pool and the dining room west of this. The kitchen was behind the living room at the base of the west wing where servants' quarters were also situated. To the east were the master bedroom and dressing room. A driveway passed under the two wings along the north side of the main house and connected two streets that defined the main yard. In the 1950s, the house was subdivided, the bedroom wing from the living room, which split the house almost in half.

The two-storey house had the main

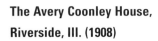

The Avery Coonley House,
Riverside, Ill. (1908)

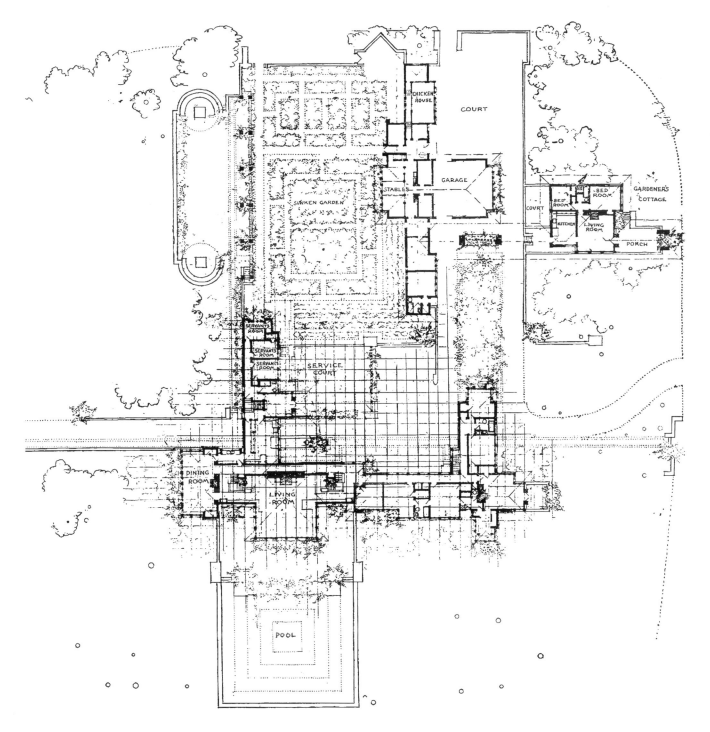

rooms on the second level, providing a wonderful view of the river and a children's playroom was located below the 24 x 27ft (7.3 x 8.2m) living room. The planning placed the two stairways just beyond the view from the living room and between the living and dining room on the west and the living room and the bedroom wing to the east. Skylights above each stairway spilled light into the living room and the hall and ceiling lights in the living room were placed behind decorative wooden lightscreens or grilles, providing filtered light after dark. Light bulbs were also placed behind the screens above the stairs.

The interior was a total Wright concept. He designed all the furniture, carpets, lighting, table runners and draperies and there was a unified colour scheme. The honey-gold quarter-sawn oak of the trim, floors and furniture was repeated in the borders of the carpets and the ceilings were a sheepskin beige which was repeated in the centre of the carpets. The plaster panels in the walls varied in colour from room to room, the dining room being a deep red, the living room green, and the bedrooms blue. The lime green of the art-glass windows, along with all the colours of the rooms, were reflected in the carpets used in each room, and the proportions of colours

used varied with the size of the room as well as the colour of the plaster. Little of these colours remain in the building today but are held in the Prairie Archives that contain the original yarn samples, along with the full sized carpet drawings. The house could be rescued and brought back to its original form, given a little elbow grease and an injection of money.

Walter V. Davidson of Buffalo, New York was another employee of the Larkin Company. His house was the last executed for associates of the company, as well as the most different, and is several blocks from the Barton and Martin houses. The house's orientation

OPPOSITE
Plan of the Avery Coonley House, Riverside, Ill. (1908)

ABOVE, RIGHT and LEFT
The Avery Coonley House (Interior), Riverside, Ill. (1908)

LEFT
The gardener's cottage

The Walter V. Davidson House, Buffalo, New York (1908)

on its lot is unusual because the living room does not face the street but looks out to the side. A later house was built within several feet of the storey-and-a-half living room windows making for an awkward situation. It is one of a group with living rooms of similar design, all designed and built within a few years of one another around 1908. The disposition of the rooms is similar in many ways to those of the Willits house designed many years earlier. The living room is situated at the front and centre, the dining room to one side and a porch to the other with the kitchen and bedrooms in the wing opposite to the

The Isabel Roberts House, River Forest, III. (1908)

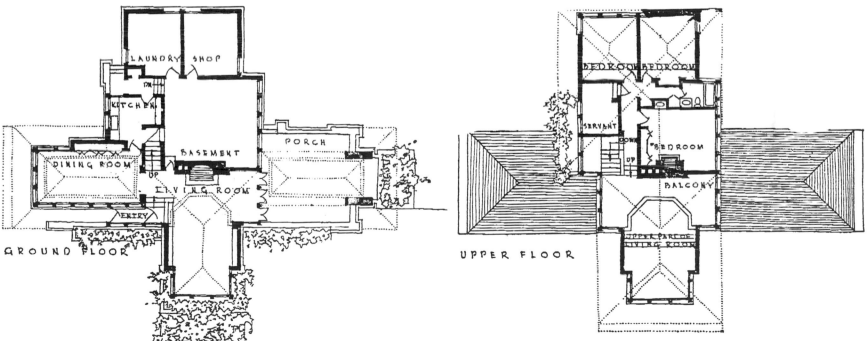

RIGHT and BELOW
**The Robert W. Evans House,
Chicago, Ill. (1908)**

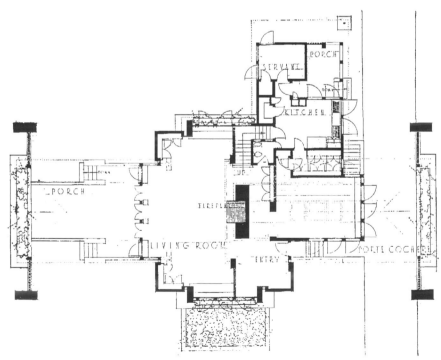

living room, to the rear, or in the case of the Davidson house, with a view to the street. This may have been the point of the re-orientation and the decision to place the living room to the side. In each of these tall living-roomed houses, the art glass was of a rather simple diamond pattern, the diamonds being wider than tall, and might even be described as lying on their sides.

The living rooms have tall windows across their entire fronts and turning back onto the sides. Adjacent to these were walls often containing bookcases and above these strings of clerestory windows at the top of the walls. Wide openings at the junctions of the dining room and low

doors to the porch are adjacent to the brick fireplace. The fireplace is at the centre of the house and opposite the tall windows and the brick face is simple iron-spot Roman brick with a plain limestone mantle. In the case of the Davidson house, above the fireplace and overlooking the living room are windows from the bedroom while in other houses of this type there is a balcony that overlooks the living room. In the dining room is a built-in oak breakfront cabinet, some of the doors having diamond-paned art-glass windows similar in pattern but on a smaller scale to the large windows.

In 1908, in River Forest, a similar

arrangement was used by one of Wright's office associates, Isabel Roberts, and her mother, Mary, who owned and earned income from property in the area.

The **Isabel Roberts House** is smaller than the Davidson and both were of stucco. The Roberts house was resurfaced in brick many years after the initial construction and Wright was called in by later owners to remodel the building when he introduced lapped boards for the ceilings, mahogany built-in cabinets in the dining room and a balcony. The diamond windows were retained. The Roberts house has the distinction of having a tree growing through the roof of the porch off the living room.

Contrary to popular belief, Isabel Roberts was not related to Charles E. Roberts or to either of Wright's clients from Kankakee, the Hickox and Bradley families. She was an architect in her own right and her talent and position

OPPOSITE
**The G.C. Stockman House,
Mason City, Iowa (1908)**
This is in its original location

LEFT
**The William H. Copeland
House, Oak Park, Ill. (1909)**
A remodelling of an earlier
brick house

in Wright's Oak Park office has been largely ignored and underestimated.

Perched at the top of a ridge in far south Chicago is the **Robert W. Evans House** which stands large in its imposing site which is over 250ft (76m) wide. Like the Davidson house in Buffalo, the entrance leads past the dining room windows but, unlike it, the basis for the

Evans design is the *Ladies' Home Journal* four-square design. The central pavilion is divided into the now familiar three sections, the living room occupying half of it and the remaining two quarters being the kitchen and the dining room. Bedrooms are above via a wide, well lit staircase at the rear. The square that defines the centre of the house is larger

than most of the other examples of this building type. Off the centre of the living room, which would be to the left of the front of the house, is a large porch that balances the entry and dining room of the other side.

This house was also fitted with Wright-designed built-in and free-standing furniture. Some of the examples

The Laura Gale House, Oak Park, Ill. (1909)

were used in other houses and there were some unique pieces. Unfortunately, all of this original furniture was sold off or removed from the house by subsequent owners, one of whom added a layer of synthetic stone to the front surfaces of the house using adhesive to stick it to the rough stucco below.

Another house perched on a high point of the neighbourhood is the 1908 **E.A. Gilmore House** of Madison, Wisconsin. Unlike most of Wright's other Prairie designs that are low and wide, the Gilmore house appears quite tall. It is an optical illusion as the house itself is very horizontal and has a stucco wall extending from the first floor, adding to the illusion. The wide overhangs and the prow at the front of the house give it the appearance of an aircraft which has led to it being nicknamed 'The Airplane House'.

The Gilmore house interior is unique in the Wright oeuvre. The living room and dining room are joined by a common ceiling but divided by a plaster half-wall topped by close-set spindles which stop before reaching the ceiling. This partition has a bench built into the living room side at the simple brick fireplace. The entry and main stairway is larger and more prominent than most

of Wright's other work and is located on the north-west corner of the house and, given the weather in Madison, this may be the reason for its brightness.

One of the last of Wright's designs based on the *Ladies' Home Journal* four-square design was the **Dr. G.C. Stockman House** of Mason City, Iowa, built in 1908. There are no documents describing how Wright met Stockman, but it was very likely through an introduction by another Wright client in Mason City. Wright was at work designing a large building for the main town square that included a bank and a hotel and the Stockman house was built on a lot just a few blocks from this. It was moved to a site further north and east of the original site near a

development designed by Wright's associate, Walter Burley Griffin, named Rock Crest and Rock Glen where it was reworked. The Stockman house has an internal breakdown where the living room comprises half the first floor. To the left is a porch wing, while on the second floor are the bedrooms. The original site had the house facing north, though in the new one it faces west.

Wright took on many remodelling jobs for his neighbours in Oak Park and by 1909 he was firmly established as one of the most creative designers and architects of the modern era. Most architects would not have considered undertaking such projects but Wright may have been under pressure to accept because **Dr. W.H. Copeland** was

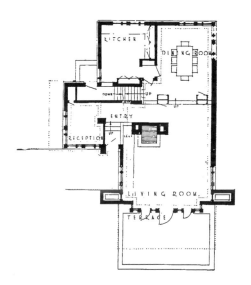

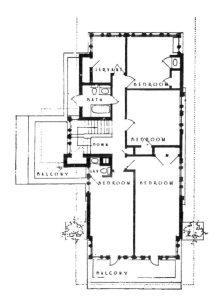

a neighbour. Remodelling is restrictive in many ways but also forces the architect to consider non-formulaic solutions. In work involving a new structure, the architect can pre-set the heights and the room sizes, but in the Copeland house Wright had to deal with a tall brick Victorian house and attempt to convert it to fit his own precepts, which was quite a task. The interior rooms are very awkward and the proportion of the trim does little to help modify the effect. The final appearance is not as successful as it would have been had he had complete control, as was the case with the Copeland garage, which is a successful design and very accessible from the street. The Copeland house is three houses south of Wright's own and just north of the Heurtley house on Forest Avenue in Oak Park.

The first piece of real estate Wright ever bought was from E.O. Gale, the father of Thomas Gale. It was Thomas and his brother Walter who obtained Wright's services for three houses in the block, across the street from his own house in Oak Park. Unfortunately, Thomas Gale died young and his widow, Laura, no longer requiring such a large house, asked Wright for a much more modest design in the same neighbourhood. Wright was given one of

The J. Kibben Ingalls
House, River Forest, Ill.
(1909)

ABOVE, LEFT and RIGHT
**The Meyer May House,
Grand Rapids, Mich. (1909)**

the smallest lots in Oak Park and designed a very modern, compact house. Unlike most of the other Prairie houses, the **Laura Gale House** did not have a pitched roof with wide overhangs, but a flat roof with minimal overhang. It has piers that rise from grade to the second-floor window sill, each of these piers supporting a wooden flower urn. The interior arrangement of the living and dining rooms is likewise unique, the two spaces being defined by large cases as well as stairs that elevate the dining area. Large doors open off the front of the living room onto a walled porch and above it is a cantilever containing the walled porch off the bedrooms. Some have compared this with the more famous Fallingwater but there are few similarities

other than flat roofs and cantilevers.

The grandson of J. Kibben Ingalls of River Forest ran one of the largest architectural bookstores in America, located just off the beach in Santa Monica, near Los Angeles. The **Ingalls House** was built in 1909 and is another unique design. The house is symmetrical and centred on the living room and front porch. To one side is a very small dining room with an oversized built-in breakfront cabinet, opposite which is the tiny entrance. There are three bedrooms on

the second floor and the family apparently feared tuberculosis. At this time, the treatment recommended was sunshine and fresh air; consequently, every living space in the Ingalls house has three exposures allowing for a maximum of light and air. The broad, hipped roofs make the building appear smaller than its actual dimensions.

The **Meyer May House**, built in 1909, appears to have been largely designed by Wright's assistant, Marion Mahony, the second woman to have achieved a degree

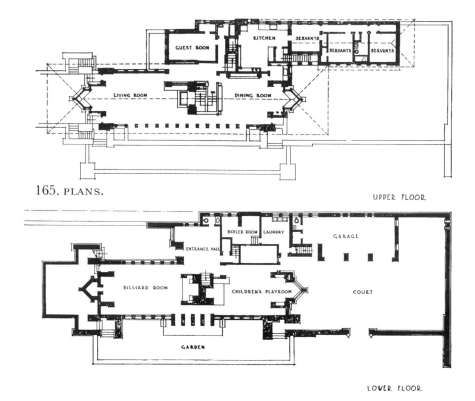

165. PLANS.

UPPER FLOOR

LOWER FLOOR

ABOVE and OPPOSITE
The Frederick C. Robie House, Chicago, Ill. (1909)

in architecture from the Massachusetts Institute of Technology. It has delicate lines and unusual architectural features which include a second-floor window projection, copper sheetwork at the living room windows and unusual room proportions and arrangements. May was the owner of a clothing store and probably became acquainted with Wright's work as a result of his many trips to Chicago. He was an innovator in the display of retail clothing and did well in business. The house had a full complement of furniture, both built-in and

free-standing, together with carpets and draperies, and there was a mural painted in the first-floor hall. The house had undergone many alterations and changes in 80 years before it was purchased and renovated by a large Grand Rapids furniture company, but is not open to the public on a regular basis. Reproductions have been placed throughout the house making the interior appear authentically convincing.

One of the most famous of Wright's houses is the **Frederick C. Robie House** which is located at the University of

Chicago campus near the site of the Colombian Exposition and World's Fair of 1893. This fair was one of the most elaborate, incorporating waterways bordered by white classical buildings with Italian gondolas sailing by. It was a most impressive presentation but was in opposition to the progressiveness of Chicago architecture at the time. Wright saw buildings at this fair that affected him throughout his life but at the same time consolidated his modernist tendencies, which was in part due to his employer at the time, Louis Sullivan. Designed by

RIGHT and OPPOSITE

The Frederick C. Robie House, Chicago, Ill. (1909)

Adler & Sullivan, the Transportation Building was virtually the only major exposition building that was non-classical and non-white.

Robie was a manufacturer who had worked for his father until his death, whereupon he took over the business making machines and parts. Of the items produced, some were bicycles and it is said that Robie did not consider there to be much of a future in bicycles and sold up to another local manufacturer, Ignaz Schwinn. The business inherited by Robie was not a healthy one and great hardship was suffered through mismanagement, the stress of which caused the break-up of his marriage. His Wright-designed house was sold just a few years later.

The house, as was mentioned earlier, was a development of the Tomek in nearby Riverside. Given that Wright began with the Tomek and after working on it produced the Robie house, one wishes that this sequence could have been applied to other house designs to see what a second generation of a house such as the Willits would have become.

The second level contains the main rooms, the living and dining rooms forming the front of the building; from the outside it is difficult to determine

BELOW and OPPOSITE

The Frederick C. Robie House, Chicago, III. (1909)

where one ends and the other begins. Inside, they are divided by the mass of the brick fireplace and defined by the ascending stairs from the main rear entrance. The kitchen is located at the back and above the garages to the right with bedrooms located on the top floor.

There are several unusual engineering features present in the house which include a steel support in the prow at each end of the living room level. This post holds a cross member that then supports two very long C-channels that run the length of the entire roof. This C-channel is what defines the change in ceiling level in the living and dining rooms. It is supported at about its mid-point by the extreme outside edges of the fireplace. The brick balcony wall for the living and dining rooms acts like a beam rather than resting on its structural supports.

Heating is provided by radiators which are set into concrete depressions in the floor in front of each of the sets of balcony doors and are covered by metal grilles. Wright designed a progressive system for venting the attic spaces and drawing the hot summer air out. A simple wooden door closes and contains the heat in winter.

The house was fitted out with a full suite of interior appointments, most of which are now gone. A wonderful free-standing cantilever couch was designed for the living room that went with small tabourets for tea, which were used before what we now know as coffee tables were developed. Custom rugs were made that varied the pattern between the living and dining rooms but kept the same theme.

While Wright was out of the country with Mamah Cheney, construction of the Robie house was completed and to budget, which was $58,000. This was an amazing feat given the level of detailing and custom fittings manufactured for the house.

Before Wright's European departure, the design was developed for the E.P. Irving House in downstate Decatur, Illinois and the house was built in 1910. The three-part room layout was again used here with the same three rooms, dining, living room and library facing the street. A long hall ran behind the living room fireplace in a similar fashion to that of the Coonley house.

More unique furniture was designed for the Irvings and included an eccentric composition that incorporated a resting couch and a desk as a single unit. Wright designed the case of a grand piano for the large living room but unfortunately it has since been lost.

Family members tell of a meeting between Wright and the Rev. J.R. Zeigler of Frankfort, Kentucky on a boat during a trans-Atlantic crossing in 1910. The problem with this is that the dates of their trips do not appear to coincide.

RIGHT and OPPOSITE
**The Jessie R. Zeigler
House, Frankfort, Kent.
(1910)**

Exactly how they met remains a mystery, as do several features of the **Zeigler House**, its basis being the *Ladies' Home Journal* design. Like the Laura Gale house there is a walled front porch off the front of the living room. The centrally located fireplace has a glazed cabinet that runs around the brickwork at the ceiling and has lights inside that appear to be original to the construction. The cabinet is far above normal sight lines and no one has come up with a reasonable explanation of its function. Wright visited the house in the early 1950s and was asked to explain it, to which he replied that no matter what it was, it was the first of its kind.

Frank Lloyd Wright left his practice in the hands of another architect, Herman von Holst, for a defined period of time while he was in Germany from 1909. He felt there should be a sense of continuity when looking after the interests of clients of a professional, and he knew he would return. There is no evidence of any correspondence between Wright and von Holst or that any of the clients that Wright left behind corresponded with him. Wright did not leave his work behind, he took it with him in preparation for the large Wasmuth portfolio of his past designs. He needed to focus himself and determine the perfect view of each building and how to present them to their best effect.

Wright also made alterations to the valley by erecting dams, the first of which was below the drafting room and was to provide electricity for the complex. Another, toward the centre of the valley, resulted in tranquil lakes that could be enjoyed in all seasons. The buildings are still in use by

Wright's school and Foundation and there are tours around it during the summer months. It is one of the most beautiful places on earth.

The **Oscar Balch House** was one of the first of the flat-roofed houses, its proportions taller than earlier houses. Balch

was one of two partners in an Oak Park decorating firm, Pebbles & Balch, for whom Wright had designed a shop in 1907. The first-floor plan is very similar to that of the Cheney House in its three-part layout consisting of library, living room and dining room, and the spaces are differentiated by

RIGHT
The William B. Greene House, Aurora, Ill. (1912)

OPPOSITE
The Harry S. Adams House, Oak Park, Ill. (1913)

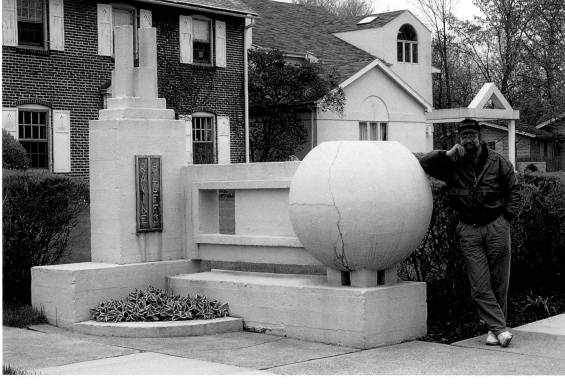

before its demolition, and was crated and shipped to New York. Ten years after, the museum hired restoration architect, Thomas A. Heinz, to reconstruct the living room inside the new American wing. This is now the most visited of all Wright's buildings and is one of the most popular of the Museum's permanent exhibits.

Wright was never one to easily discard a good idea and continued to develop the elevations of the basic plan first used in the *Ladies' Home Journal* Fireproof House for $5,000, used in its original form in the 1907 Hunt house. The façade is given added

depth by the piers of the windows on the street elevation as well as on the other sides. The building is much smaller than it appears, however, because of these architectural extensions.

Sherman Booth acted as an attorney on behalf of Wright for several years and first commissioned a house for himself in 1911, though it was a much more elaborate scheme than the one finally built in 1915, the land having been purchased in the name of Elizabeth, Sherman's wife. The Booth scheme involved not only several residential designs but also a new town hall and library and it

OPPOSITE ABOVE LEFT and RIGHT
The Ravine Bluffs Development corner markers (1915)

OPPOSITE BELOW
The First Sherman Booth House, Glencoe, Ill. (1911)

LEFT
The Second Sherman Booth House, Glencoe, Ill. (1915)

The J.M. Compton House, Ravine Bluffs Development, Glencoe, Ill. (1915)

Meadow Road, one gets a true idea of what a town designed by Wright might feel like. At one time, two of the houses were owned by Booth's brother-in-law, Herbert Angster, also a Wright client. The reason for Angster's involvement is unclear but it may have been a real estate investment or to help in the financing of Booth's work.

There are many Wright designs overlooking Lake Michigan in the four states that border this body of water, Wisconsin, Illinois, Indiana and Michigan and **Joseph J. Bagley** built his Wright design at Grand Beach, Michigan. However, the house has been altered considerably and little of Wright's genius manages to come through. It is not known if this Bagley was related to Wright's earlier 1890 Hinsdale client of the same name.

A larger and more elaborate development of the 1907 *Ladies' Home Journal* Fireproof House for $5,000 is the **Frederick C. Bogk House** of Milwaukee. There are several interior departures and probably the most dramatic is the change of of levels between rooms, resulting in a welcome height addition to the living room and a better view from the dining room, making it feel less cramped. The roofed porches which can be seen on the Booth Ravine Bluffs houses are small, tiled-floored sun traps on the south sides of the buildings but the Bogk scheme has a small outside

The J.M. Compton House, Ravine Bluffs Development, Glencoe, Ill. (1915)

The S.J. Gilfillan House, Ravine Bluffs Development, Glencoe, Ill. (1915)

The Joseph J. Bagley House, Grand Beach, Mich. (1916)

balcony above it leading from a bedroom.

From the outside one might expect the living room to be dark because of the deep-set casement windows. This is not the case: in fact, the living room is very bright, the thin, vertical slit windows at the sides of the major windows being responsible for the additional light. There are similar windows in both the magazine design and the first realization in the Stephen Hunt house of La Grange, 1907.

The large sculptural figures on the building's face are unique in Wright's residential work. Each depicts a winged man holding two blocks before him. The abstraction follows Wright's work at the Midway Gardens in Chicago that preceded it by just a few years and many of the architectural features used in the Bogk house were incorporated in the Imperial Hotel of Tokyo, just a few years afterwards.

There are four buildings in the **Arthur**

Richards Duplex Apartments, all situated next to one another. They have opposite-handed plans making two sets of two buildings, each of them costing $4,500 from the City Real Estate Company. They were the first to be constructed using Wright's invention, the American Ready-Cut System, a company founded by Richards, and all the buildings were originally stucco-surfaced. Rudolph Schindler was working with Wright at the time these drawings were prepared and

the buildings seem to have influenced Schindler's work for many years after.

At the west end of this block were two other Richards Company Wright designs, one being a cottage, the other a bungalow. Both of these structures are constructed using the same pre-cut lumber system as the four duplexes. The bungalow is the most repeated of the pre-cut system and like its taller neighbours, also consists of a wooden frame with stucco over wood lath. The planning is quite free and is defined by the familiar wooden trim strips that occur, connecting the heads of all the doors and windows.

As with all of these Milwaukee American System buildings, there are long strips of windows on all sides and the interior planning is as good as the exterior appearance. The fireplace is at the outside wall in contrast to nearly every other Wright house design, where it is situated near the centre of the building. The living room and dining room are one zone and the bathroom and two bedrooms form another; it is

The Arthur Richards Duplex Apartments, Milwaukee, Wisc. (1916)

The Frederick C. Bogk
House, Milwaukee, Wisc.
(1916)

through the use of these zones that economy of lumber and construction is effected.

Frederick Bogk was apparently related to **Arthur Munkwitz** and they both lived in the same neighbourhood, as did their Wright clients of the time. This is also where Munkwitz's now-demolished 1916 duplex apartments were built in near west Milwaukee. They were removed in 1973 by the City of Milwaukee in order to widen the street in front. Munkwitz and other members

of his family were involved in real estate all over Milwaukee and this seemed to be but one venture, certainly the one for which he will be remembered.

Another family business was the Badger Nail Company. These were modest apartments but well designed with all the modern facilities installed.

Stephen M. B. Hunt moved from his Prairie house of 1907, in La Grange, Illinois to Oshkosh, a small town in central

Wisconsin. This second Hunt house was recently identified as one of the American Systems bungalows though Hunt never lived in the house and the property was apparently rented out.

Henry Allen was one of the most interesting of Wright's clients, having become Governor of Kansas after a long and successful career as the editor of an influential newspaper. He became an important political spokesman and was close

BELOW

The Arthur Munkwitz Duplexes, Milwaukee, Wisc. (1916)

These were torn down by the City of Milwaukee in order to widen the street

OPPOSITE
**The Stephen M.B. Hunt
House, Oshkosh, Wisc.
(1917)**

LEFT
**The Henry J. Allen
House, Wichita, Kans.
(1917)**

to several presidents. He was well along in
years when he asked Wright for a design and
in many ways the result is similar to the
earlier Little house for Wayzata. The living
room had windows on the longitudinal sides
but it was jointed at its connection to the
dining room and the remainder of the house.
This elbow, and a wall that ran along the
sidewalk, formed a courtyard with the garage

and completed the rectangle. Within this
courtyard was what resembled an oriental
terrace and pool. The house has been well
maintained and is open to the public. It is
situated in the small town of Wichita, Kansas,
and is a true Prairie house.

Aline Barnsdall's father was one of the
earliest Americans to drill and discover
petroleum in Pennsylvania and amassed

quite a fortune which he passed on to his
daughter upon his death. Aline was not
interested in business, but in the arts, and
was active in Chicago's theatrical scene
where she had met Wright in the teens. She
wanted a theatre of her own but, while
travelling, decided to relocate to Los Angeles
where she bought an olive orchard which
included a small hill at its centre. She hired

The Aline Barnsdall (Hollyhock) House, Los Angeles, Calif. (1920)

Wright to design not only her house but also accommodation for artists and theatre personnel who would service the two theatres Wright was to design. Wright did design the large house for Aline as well as two studio residences and the beginning of a kindergarten for her daughter and the neighbourhood children.

Los Angeles in 1920 was a city full of energy. Aline was an active member of the community and met many others who supported her efforts. However, other interests frustrated and distracted her from completing her master plan though Wright did design another house for Beverly Hills, which was never built.

The **Barnsdall House** follows the line of the Imperial Hotel and the Allen house and

was built around a courtyard. Since Los Angeles is a desert, the thinking at the time was that harsh sunlight was something to be avoided and the house was developed to keep it out. The windows are therefore small and deep-set and the colours of the interior are a shady umber and purple. Initially, Wright developed three schemes, including one with low-pitched roofs and broad eaves in the Prairie mode. The final one was a modern structure which many feel has overtones of the Mayan culture. However, although it is evocative of the style, it is not an imitation. The ornament is an abstraction

of the hollyhock which is said to have been Aline's favourite flower and is used in the band that surrounds the house, as well as the column capitals and the art-glass window patterns.

The courtyard was occasionally used for theatrical events, with the audience seated in the courtyard and the players acting on the roofs and terraces, while at other times the arrangement would be reversed.

The living room is the largest interior space and is filled with two opposite-handed pieces of furniture, which could possibly be described as couches with tables and lamps

attached to them and these were pulled close to the fireplace. At the fireplace hearth was a deep but not large pool. It was to have been connected with the upper pool at the back of the courtyard and the larger stepped pool outside the front of the living room. There were tall-backed chairs for the living room tables, while for the dining room, which proportionally seems too small, were tall-backed chairs and a matching table which were an important departure from earlier dining sets: it was clear that Wright was embarking upon a new direction in design.

After having obtained a Wright design for

ABOVE LEFT and RIGHT
The Aline Barnsdall (Hollyhock) House, Los Angeles, Calif. (1920)

RIGHT and OPPOSITE

The Alice Millard House (La Miniatura), Pasadena, Calif. (1923)

their Highland Park, Illinois house, George and Alice Millard moved to Pasadena where George died soon after and Alice took charge of the business dealing in fine books and antiques. She returned to Wright for another house, who developed a revolutionary system of decorative moulded concrete blocks for the new house. He assisted with the choice of the site, suggesting she sell her flat rectangular builder's site and purchase a less costly one that no one else wanted at the bottom of a small ravine in the same development near the Pasadena Rose Bowl. The **Alice Millard House** is cubic and the concrete blocks were often pierced, allowing light to enter; there are operable casement windows on the interior to regulate air flow entering the house. The living room consists of a full two storeys and has a balcony overlooking it, the bedrooms looking north up the ravine. Below the house, a pond was constructed to reflect the house and the many weeping willows on the site.

In 1923 Wright was to produce one of his most efficient houses for **Dr. John Storer** of Los Angeles. The plan for it had already been presented to an earlier client who decided not to build it. Unfortunately, the plan only works on a site that has a significant pitch to it, but the site of the Storer house provides a view across Hollywood unattainable to most. Using a concrete block system improved from the one used on the Millard house, steel rods

RIGHT
**The Alice Millard House
(La Miniatura), Pasadena,
Calif. (1923)**

FAR RIGHT and OPPOSITE
**The John Storer House,
Los Angeles, Calif.(1923)**

have been added. This improves the ability of the house to survive earthquakes that are prevalent in the California area. One might have expected grey concrete to be unacceptable in a residence; however, the decomposed granite used as an aggregate adds a warm yellow cast and, combined with a red-hued wood, the concrete becomes perfectly suitable.

Samuel and Harriet Freeman were members of a progressive artistic community, Harriet being a dancer who might be classified as a performance artist today, while Samuel was a successful jeweller. Harriet was related to the Lovells who had built their

Neutra house to the north across a small ravine in Los Angeles. When the Freemans died, they left their house to a public trust that eventually passed to the University of Southern California which also has the famous Gamble house of Pasadena.

The plan of the **Freeman House** was largely dictated by its site, a small piece of very steep terrain. The house rises over three storeys, though only two are used as living spaces. This was the first of Wright's buildings to have what are now his famous corner windows, windows which have no supports or divisions and that have mitred glass; these open up the

corner of a room like no other device.

The last and the largest of the California concrete block houses is the 1924 **Charles Ennis House**, in Los Angeles. With the exception of the guest and servants' quarters, the house can be said to be a one-bedroomed arrangement. The house measures over 3,000sq ft (914m²) on a single floor – a very large house made to appear larger than its dimensions by the extensions that include several terraces, a parking area and the servants' quarters at the far west end of the building. The Ennis house is often included in the Wright buildings thought to be based on historic styles, in this case,

The Samuel Freeman House, Los Angeles, Calif. (1924)

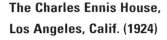

The Charles Ennis House, Los Angeles, Calif. (1924)

Mayan. This misconception may stem from the building's tapered walls and the hoods over the large deep-set windows, as well as the richly textured wall surfaces. The interior spaces are well defined, each having their own volumes expressed on the exterior. The orientation of each room is clearly towards the magnificent views of the city of Los Angeles and the Pacific Ocean beyond. Sadly, the large earthquakes which have wracked Los Angeles in the past several years have taken their toll on the Ennis house and, already weakened in earlier tremors, large sections of the

surfaces of the blocks have become loose.

The Ennis house may well be one of Wright's best known designs as it has been used in several Hollywood movies, among them *Bladerunner* and *Grand Canyon*, as well as in television commercials and magazine advertisements. These mostly take the form of subtle background shots, but they have been seen by millions.

Graycliff, built on Lake Erie, south of Buffalo, was Wright's next residential work and came three years after the Ennis house. The site is very long, extending from the high lakeside bluff to a quiet road that

follows the lake. It was Darwin D. Martin's wife who decided that they needed a summer house at Derby, New York in 1927. The house was built very close to the edge of the bluff and provides wonderful views of the lake. The house has none of the Prairie style, with low-pitched roofs and wide eaves. It does have an interesting mix of stone on the lower section and stucco above. As with the Storer house, Graycliff has tall windows on the two long sides and the bedrooms are on the second floor and strung along a hallway oriented with views to the lake. There are smaller outbuildings that are more unusual and interesting than the main house itself. The furniture was designed for the house and most of it remains *in situ* to this day. Graycliff has been adopted by an intelligent and energetic group of New Yorkers and is open for tours.

Richard Lloyd Jones, editor of the *Tulsa Tribune* in Oklahoma, asked his cousin, Frank Lloyd Wright, for a house design in 1929. The house was built by a long term associate of Wright's, Paul R. Mueller. Mueller had been an engineer in the Adler & Sullivan office where the two had met, and had been the contractor on many of Wright's buildings. The construction was observed by a young Tulsa architect, Bruce Goff, who had been an admirer of Wright's work for many years. The house is constructed of smooth-sided concrete blocks,

RIGHT
**Graycliff, The Darwin D.
Martin House, Derby,
New York (1927)**

OPPOSITE
**The Richard LLoyd Jones
House, Tulsa, Okla. (1929)**

similar to those used in California a few years earlier. The concept of the house is different, however, the concrete blocks being 16in (41cm) on each side and they are set 16 inches apart, all along the outside walls. This makes the walls appear to have vertical stripes which at first seems odd but is hardly noticeable after a few minutes spent in the house. The planning of the Jones house is along the lines of the earlier Allen house of Wichita where the walls and garage define a courtyard with a pool at its centre. There were a few pieces of furniture designed for the house that remain with it.

In 1929 the Stock Market crashed, causing a long-term depression. However, employees of the major universities managed to hold down their jobs and one of the deans at the University of Minnesota, **Malcom M. Willey**, commissioned Wright to design for him a house. The first scheme was

The Malcolm E. Willey House, Minneapolis, Minn. (1933)

rejected and the second, a more conservative but equally interesting solution, was built on the south side of a hill in 1933. It was a two-bedroomed house with the living and dining rooms combined and the brick used on the walls was also used for the floor. There were large clerestories and a wood ceiling trim,

making the house seem larger than its actual dimensions. The most famous of all Wright's work is unquestionably the Edgar Kaufmann weekend house, better known as **Fallingwater**. It was built in 1936 for the owner of a large retail store in Pittsburgh. Kaufmann's son, Edgar Jnr., who had read

Wright's autobiography, became a member of the Taliesin Fellowship, and encouraged his father to contact Wright. The two men got along well and Kaufmann asked him to design a house. Wright visited the site, and after a great deal of thought produced the presentation drawings himself. However,

The Edgar Kaufmann House (Fallingwater), Mill Run, Penn. (1936)

RIGHT
The Edgar Kaufmann House (Fallingwater), Mill Run, Penn. (1936)

OPPOSITE
The Abby Beecher Roberts House, Marquette, Mich. (1936)

somewhere along the way, Kaufmann began to question the structural integrity of the design and Wright withdrew from the project for a time; but they were eventually able to work out their differences and the house was completed.

The stone used in the house was quarried from the property and the large rock that protrudes from the floor in the living room is original to its location and remains unaltered. A guest house was added

a few years after the main house was completed and a full set of furniture was designed; however, Kaufmann did not like the dining chairs and substituted Italian three-legged ones instead.

Kaufmann died and left the house and his fortune to his only son who donated the house and some of the family land to the Western Pennsylvania Conservancy Organization. Kaufmann Jnr. remained active in the administration of his gift and was well

pleased with the stewardship which continues. The house is visited throughout the year.

John Lautner had joined the Taliesin Fellowship and his grandmother, **Abby Beecher Roberts**, of Marquette, Michigan, followed his career, meeting Wright in the process and obtaining her Wright design in 1936. The three-bedroomed house has an unusual feature in that the living room and the terrace are set at 45° off axis. As with

The Paul Hanna (Honeycomb) House, Stanford (Palo Alto), Calif. (1937)

Graycliff, the house uses a mix of materials, combining both brick and stucco.

Undoubtedly the house with the most unusual plan and construction technique is the **Paul R. Hanna House** of Stanford, California, 1937. It is based on interlocking octagons resembling a honeycomb. The Hannas had read books by and about Wright while teaching at Columbia University, New York, and eventually took a position at

Stanford where they were able to secure a piece of land for a house on university property. Wright sent the plans and asked the Hannas to study the drawings for a few days when he would call and explain them further. The Hannas had complete faith in Wright's abilities and acted as their own general contractors as no one else felt able to take on such a complex project.

It was necessary for Wright's design to

accommodate changes which would occur throughout the lives of the clients and in parallel with the life of the house. As a result, the playroom became a formal dining room and the bedrooms home offices for the two professors after the children had left home. Wright designed the furniture for the house which Paul built in a workshop on the property.

The building had been constructed on a

The Herbert Jacobs I House, Madison, Wisc. (1937)

wood screwed to them, making a total thickness of over 2in (5cm) with no studs, a form of construction which is not allowed in the building codes of today. The planning was as innovative as the construction. The living room would be large and tall with a wide opening to the dining and kitchen areas. A 90° wing, also on a concrete slab, would contain the bedrooms. This was to become a popular design used in many regenerations over 20 years, and is thought to be the first Usonian house.

Another native of Wisconsin, **Herbert Johnson**, had recently weathered a complex construction project with the building of Wright's design for his administration building, the Johnson Wax company. The house was a modern development of the Willits house with its pinwheel arrangement and was on a very large piece of property that once held Johnson's airstrip. He wanted his children to be able to watch his landings and takeoffs and for this purpose had a glass addition made to the roof. The house can be considered a one-storey building although there are rooms below the master bedroom wing, unlike the Willits house. Here, each wing defines a separate function: the master bedroom, children's rooms, garages and services which includes the kitchen and servants' rooms. The central pavilion in some parts is two-storeyed and appears to be closed in from the outside and very open from the

OPPOSITE and LEFT
**The Herbert F. Johnson
House (Wingspread),
Wind Point, Wisc. (1937)**

concrete slab into which the honeycomb grid was etched, with brick piers, while some of the walls were made of wood. On this grid the wall pattern would be established. After it was finished, the Hannas were convinced that the next house of this type they built would be much easier because of what they had already learned from the process.

Wright was full of ideas now that his second career was taking off so successfully.

He had made the acquaintance of a Madison newspaperman, **Herbert Jacobs**, who asked Wright to produce a challenging design for him. Jacobs was a family man of modest means and told Wright that he could spend no more than $5,000 for the house, being already in possession of a site on the edge of Madison. A new system was developed by Wright for the house's wooden walls which were to have a plywood centre and solid

**The Ben Rebhuhn House,
Long Island, New York
(1937)**

and generous grounds serve this function admirably. They are meticulously maintained and a pleasure to visit.

The **Ben Rebhuhn House**, Great Neck, Long Island, New York, 1937 is the missing link between the Prairie and the later Usonian designs. (USONIA stands for United States of North America and is describing small, free-standing houses for 'true Americans'.) The low-pitched roofs with broad overhangs are evident, as are the clean red brick and cypress cladding. The planning is a mix as well, the Isabel Roberts tall living room being in evidence along with an open carport at the rear.

It is rather difficult to determine just what Wright's original intentions were for the **Andrew Armstrong House** as there have

LEFT
The Andrew F. Armstrong House, Ogden Dunes, Ind. (1939)

BELOW
The Bernard Schwartz House, Two Rivers, Wisc. (1939)

inside. The reason for the differing perceptions are the deep piers that frame the tall doors and windows of the four sides. From the inside, one can see out easily while from the outside the appearance is dark and secluded as one is rarely looking in the same line as the piers and they appear closed.

Soon after Wingspread was finished, Herbert's wife died and he remarried. However, his second wife did not care for the house and a new residence was built nearby with interiors designed by T.H. Robsjohn-Gibbings. The entire complex has been donated to the Johnson Foundation to be used as a conference centre and the buildings

The Goetsch-Winkler
House, Okemos, Mich.
(1939)

been many alterations to the building, including some by John H. Howe. The house faces north, into the wind, which is the direction which commands the most beautiful views of Lake Michigan, and is built in an area of sand dunes among winding paths and mature trees.

By the late 1930s, Wright was well aware of the power of the press and got another house design published. The 26 September 1938 issue of *Life* magazine featured a design

that would become the **Bernard Schwartz House** of 1939. The house was a mix of the Willey, Graycliff and Storer houses, all rolled into one. The two-sided living room of the Storer house was rescaled with larger piers between the doors and the upper-floor bedrooms, as with Graycliff, and the smooth brick and horizontal cypress boards contrast well with the textured concrete and the stone surfaces of the earlier buildings.

A progressive, liberal group of Michigan

ABOVE
The Theodore Baird House, Amherst, Mass. (1940)

LEFT
The George D. Sturges House, Brentwood Heights, Calif. (1939)

The Sidney Bazett House, Hillsborough, Calif. (1940)

State University professors decided to approach Wright concerning a small housing development for them in a town just east of Lansing in Okemos, Michigan. Once planning was under way, some dropped out after conventional financing failed to be forthcoming, leaving only **Alma Goetsch and Katherine Winkler** to follow through on their house plans and construction. It is much like the Willey plan, but the living room has windows on both sides. After retirement, the ladies moved to Arkansas and had another Taliesin apprentice, E. Fay Jones, build their next house for them.

The **George D. Sturges House** is a reworking of the first scheme presented to Malcolm Willey a few years earlier. The entire building is cantilevered above a small base, allowing for a free-flowing site. The house faces to the south with the front entry at the back and the view over the hilly Brentwood neighbourhood of Los Angeles and the Pacific Ocean is quite spectacular. The 1500-sq ft (457m²) two-bedroomed house is one of the smallest of Wright's second or Usonian period. John Lautner was the Taliesin apprentice sent to assist in the construction and went on to have a successful career of his own in Los Angeles.

Another college professor, **Theodore Baird**, built his Wright house in Amherst, Massachusetts in 1940, after struggling to raise the finance for it. The house has no

windows to the north and is set well back from the street in this small college town.

The **Sidney Bazett House** follows the same honeycomb grid established at the nearby Hanna house at Stanford a few years earlier. There is no history of construction difficulties and the Hannas were happy to contribute their expertise to the project. The Bazetts faced other problems and divorced soon after the construction was completed and sold the house to Louis Frank who still lives there. The situation of the house and the pleasant landscaping makes for well-defined rear grounds.

There is a mystery surrounding the identity of **Joseph Euchtman** of Baltimore, Maryland. Usually when a Wright design was built in a community, it became newsworthy. However, this is not the case with the Euchtman house which is identical to the Baird except that a small study was added to the end of the living room, the plan being the other way round to that of the Baird. The neighbourhood is an ordinary one but has the redeeming feature of having a beautiful creek running through it.

Lloyd Lewis was a newspaperman from Chicago who, in 1940, decided to abandon

The Joseph Euchtman
House, Baltimore,
Maryland (1940)

OPPOSITE
**The Lloyd Lewis House,
Libertyville, Ill. (1940)**

LEFT
**The John C. Pew House,
Shorewood Hills, Wisc.
(1940)**

the busy city for what was then the country, in Libertyville, Illinois. As with the Sturges house, the main rooms are lifted off the ground for practical purposes to avoid flooding, the property being adjacent to the Des Plaines river which periodically bursts its banks. This was the first house whose extensions defined the garden, and concrete strips off the living room piers made for a mud-free access.

The interior is suffused with a warm glow caused by the light reflecting off the unfinished cypress used on the ceilings and walls. Light bulbs set behind some of the ceiling boards spotlight the surface of the fireplace as well as giving general illumination to the entire living room. This house has several levels, the living room being the highest, followed by the dining room and kitchen. The bedrooms are on the lowest level.

There was a series of cantilevered and elevated buildings in the late 1930s and early 1940s, the most beautiful of all being the

John C. Pew House of 1940 in Wisconsin. It is sited on the steep south shore of Lake Mendota and the small dimensions of the living room are alleviated by the full-height glass doors, leading to the living room terrace. The windows of the north wall look out over the lake. The stone of the large piers is repeated in the central fireplace and a large rock spans the full width of the firebox opening.

After the important role filled by Fallingwater, the next most notable project in Wright's Usonian period is the **Loren Pope** (Pope-Leighy) house in Mount Vernon, Virginia, the design of which is patterned after the Jacobs house in Madison. It had no spectacular view to or from the house but it was the client, Loren Pope, who was responsible for making it so influential and important. Pope was a newspaperman in Washington, D.C. and wrote an article in *House Beautiful* magazine in which he praised the space and economy of his house's design, as well as his struggle financing it.

OPPOSITE and ABOVE
The Pope-Leighy House, Woodlawn, Virginia (1940)

RIGHT and OPPOSITE
The C. Leigh Stevens House, Auldbrass Plantation, Yemassee, S.C. (1940)

The article was so well written, and read by so many people, that Wright's practice exploded into life after the end of the Second World War and well into the 1950s. Future clients retained the article and quoted parts of it to Wright when they wrote to him asking for a house of their own and Wright just could not refuse them.

One of the most unusual structures Wright ever designed was for **Leigh Stevens** of New York who had purchased land in a lowland area near to the coast of South Carolina in the 1930s and wanted a plantation house with many outbuildings to accommodate his workers as well as implements and horses. In 1940, Wright offered him a design that included a large house based on a honeycomb but with inwardly sloping walls. The low-pitched roofs were of copper, and red brick and cedar were used throughout the property. Red colouring was added to the trowelling of the concrete floor slabs and they were waxed to a high polish. The estate has since been rescued and restored, and is occasionally open to visitors.

The last of the cantilevered raised-room houses is the 1940 **Gregor Affleck House** in Bloomfield Hills, Michigan. The site slopes to the north and is located just over a hill from the famous Cranbrook Academy designed by Wright's friend Eliel Saarinen. The main floor is on two levels and there is a basement that

RIGHT
The Gregor S. Affleck House, Bloomfield Hills, Mich. (1941)

is largely exposed above grade. In the living room is a most unusual feature, in which a short wall is open to a small pool below. One cannot view the pool without standing at the wall and looking almost straight down and must surely have been a requirement of the client.

Herbert Jacobs built one of the first of Wright's Usonian houses in 1937 in Madison, but the family soon outgrew the small house and asked Wright for a larger but equally economical one. Jacobs had plenty of time but little cash and the second building was actually the third design Wright proposed for him. This final is referred to as the **Jacobs II**

RIGHT
The Herbert Jacobs II House, Middleton, Wisc. (1943)

OPPOSITE
The Melvin Maxwell Smith House, Bloomfield Hills, Mich. (1949)

RIGHT and BELOW
The Melvin Maxwell Smith House, Bloomfield Hills, Mich. (1949)

OPPOSITE
The Douglas Grant House, Cedar Rapids, Iowa (1946)

House. It is a solar hemicycle and was built in Middleton, Wisconsin in 1943. It took a long time to complete as Jacobs and Wright decided to construct it using stone and Jacobs and his supportive wife assisted the masons, often hauling materials and sometimes laying stone themselves. The house was built against a bank of earth to the north to provide insulation as well as direct north breezes into the high bedroom windows. The bedrooms were on the second level which was supported by steel rods attached to the roof rafters. The first floor is open and only partly separated from the kitchen by a circular tower containing the

The James Edwards House, Okemos, Mich. (1949)

LEFT
The Henry J. Neils House, Minneapolis, Minn. (1950)

The Chauncey L. Griggs House, Tacoma, Wash. (1946)

whole, not as innovative or interesting as his earlier work – and this applies especially after the Second World War.

As with the Smith house, the 1946 **Douglas Grant House** of Cedar Rapids is unusual. The entrance is at the opposite end of the house from the living room and residents and visitors both need to traverse the house from one end to the other down a long descending ramp. The living room is a full two storeys high and there is no wooden siding inside or out. The stone was quarried by the clients directly from the property and there are four bedrooms and an area designated as a locker room for the children.

Lowell Walter wished to retire from his home in Des Moines to his farm at Quasqueton, Iowa, in about 1945. He was a contractor and was at the time working on the road below Taliesin when Wright came to inquire about the paving he was using, and the two became friends. The Lowell site gave Wright an opportunity to place the living and dining rooms at a 60° angle to the bedroom wing. The axis of the main view was aligned with the main rooms and the bedrooms were along the same elevation in a line toward the

The Amy Alpaugh House, Northport, Mich. (1947)

road. The view is of the Wapsinicon river and Wright also designed a two-level boathouse there.

The most surprising element of the design is the roof fascia which is of curved plaster, the curve making the roof appear thicker than it is. The other change from most of the other Usonian houses was not that there are heating pipes under the floor, or that the floor is

concrete, but that it is not poured into place but consists of concrete panels which are removable should any future problems occur. It is surprising that this is the only Wright house to use this system as the cost of cutting and replacing a poured floor is high and the appearance not particularly attractive.

Erling Brauner of Okemos was a Michigan State University professor and a

colleague of Alma Goetsch and Katherine Winkler. He collaborated with Wright and together they came up with a design for a house in 1948. It is at the end of a quiet street and makes clever use of what is a very small site. The house looks out to a lower yard at the end of a dead-end street and is constructed of concrete blocks.

Across the street, at the end of the cul-de-

RIGHT

The A.H. Bubilian House, Rochester, Minn. (1947)

BELOW

The Caroll Alsop House, Oskaloosa, Iowa (1948)

BELOW RIGHT

The Jack Lamberson House, Oskaloosa, Iowa (1948)

sac, is another Wright house built for **James Edwards**. He was a neighbour of another Okemos resident, Don Schaberg. This 1949 house also explored the use of the offset room scheme also used in the Walter house. The Edwards house is constructed of red brick and has cypress cladding.

In keeping with the theme of offsets in Wright's plans is a house for **Henry J. Neils** of Minneapolis, Minnesota. Neils was a buildings products dealer and specialized in granite, marble and architectural metals. Wright was always willing to accommodate the wishes of clients and this house is constructed of granite and has aluminium windows, one of the few examples of metal windows in the Usonian period. The house had a set of beautiful Wright-designed furniture that included a floor model of the pole lamp.

Chauncey Griggs ran a lumber business in Tacoma after graduating from Yale. The design of the house is unusual in Wright's later work, the most distinctive feature being the roof which is of a shed type – that is, with only one pitch. It has no ridge, no hips and no gables. The house is built alongside a pleasant stream which limits access to the main part of the property. The walls are of concrete block and the floor has the typical poured and scored concrete treatment.

Amy Alpaugh raised goats on her property and the human living quarters most

likely constitute the smallest house Wright ever designed. Two of the tiniest bedrooms are situated off a hallway and a person would have difficulty turning around in one of them. Despite its diminutive size, the house has one of the most picturesque sites of any Wright building, with views of Grand Traverse Bay, Lake Michigan, and some of the most beautiful timberland of the Midwest at Northport, Michigan. This house also contains an offset living room, here termed the studio or workroom.

Wright's mastery of a site is well in evidence in the **Dr. A.H. Bubilian House** of Rochester, Minnesota. The offset living and dining rooms break the composition's strict rectangularity and enhance the view to the south-east. Financial savings were achieved by altering the standard materials and methods used in the basic wall construction. The original clients lived in the house for a very long time, in fact until the 1990s.

The **Caroll Alsop House** of Oskaloosa, Iowa was built in 1948 and is one of the finest of all the Wright Usonian designs. The site is wonderful with its small lake and rolling terrain. Beautiful red brick has been used with cypress for the ceilings and window frames. The living room is a tall, large square and the slope of the roof focuses the view horizontally to the lake and the landscape beyond.

The Maynard P. Buehler House, Orinda, Calif. (1948)

It is unusual enough to have one Wright design in a small town in Iowa, but Oskaloosa has two, the Alsop and the **Jack Lamberson House**, which were built about the same time. While technically the house is not based on a triangle, in form it does appear to be triangular. The house is small but is covered by a very large roof and is also built of red brick and cypress.

The **Maynard Buehler House** of Orinda, California was built in 1948 and combines several geometric forms not found in other Wright houses, having an octagonal living room and several arched walls in the service wing, as well as one in the swimming pool. The roof of the living room is a square with a single pitched shed roof.

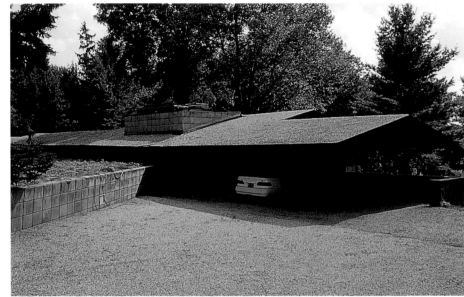

ABOVE
The Robert D. Winn House, Kalamazoo, Mich. (1948)

ABOVE RIGHT
The Eric V. Brown House, Kalamazoo, Mich. (1949)

RIGHT
The Ward McCartney House, Kalamazoo, Mich. (1949)

The Robert Levin House, Kalamazoo, Mich. (1949)

The Eric Pratt House, Galesburg, Mich. (1948)

The David I. Weisblatt House, Galesburg, Mich. (1948)

Wright was not only the designer of individual buildings, he was also asked by a group of friends, mostly employed by the Upjohn Company, to assist them in planning their community, a former orchard. They had close to 50 acres (20 hectares) and planted over 1,000 more trees. Wright conceived a plan in which an assortment of equal sized circles as individual lots for each house would allow several acres of park to be used by the residents. This area was to be named Parkwyn Village within a small city in south Michigan. Defining property lines would have become a problem with the circles and more conventional means of lot definitions were adopted. Out of the final count of 40 lots, only four would contain Wright designs.

The houses were for **Robert Winn**, **Ward McCartney**, **Eric Brown** and **Robert Levin**, and all of them were built of concrete block, the blocks being similar to those used in the Arizona Biltmore Hotel. The blocks were initially manufactured by the clients themselves at a rate of 150 blocks per day but

The Samuel Eppstein House, Galesburg, Mich. (1949)

it was soon decided to contract the task out.

The buildings were all quite modest, perhaps the most interesting being the one designed for McCartney. It was based on a diamond grid which allowed for many sharp corners and pointed closets. The extensions of the roof cantilevers were accentuated by their slim profile.

A second contemporaneous scheme was designed for another group of friends in nearby Galesburg, Michigan. Both groups knew one another and again, most were employed by the Upjohn Company to assist them in planning their community. This plan allowed for 22 circular lots and a smaller ratio of parkland within the development;

there was a curved road that was to transect the subdivision.

As with the Parkwyn Village scheme, only four Wright designs were executed at the 1948 Country Home Acres development in Galesburg and were constructed over several years from 1948 to 1950. These houses were for **Eric Pratt**, **David**

Weisblatt, **Samuel Eppstein, and Curtis Meyer**. To this day, not all the lots have been sold or used for other purposes.

The most unusual was the **Meyer House** which is similar in many ways to the Jacobs II house in its use of a partial arc of a circle and was oriented more to the north than the south, as was Jacobs II. The materials were concrete block and mahogany and Meyer kept the wood in a beautiful original condition by using a Dutch Boy product that acted as an ultraviolet light block. The wood was not sealed with varnish or shellac and had the patina of furniture for many years. The other three houses were very similar in their plans but because of the rolling site and alternative roof designs, they appear unique.

Several of the eight houses were altered or added to by Wright and his chief draftsman after Wright's death, Jack Howe. Vegetation has filled in many of the sites over the past 50 years and because the designs were never oriented to the street, they are now very difficult to see.

The site for the **Kenneth Laurent House** of Rockford, Illinois was large but had no special features that would justify the unusual geometry which Wright applied to the design. It appears that Wright was exploring alternatives in this innovative house and the client was in on the experiment and well pleased with the result.

At first glance, the **Charles Weltzheimer**

House of Oberlin, Ohio (1948) appears to be the same as many other of the 90°-angled one-storey, flat-roofed houses. In this example there are several places where the house is more than one room wide; this does not sound revolutionary but was in fact a radical departure. The roofs and the drainage from them, as well as the weight of the snow, are two reasons for keeping the cross dimensions to a minimum.

Many of the Usonian designs are thin and long, most of them having been designed in this fashion because of site or lot limitations. In the **Albert Adelman House** of 1948, the reason was privacy. The house is oriented on a diagonal across the lot and is over 150ft (45m) long. The rooms are not narrow but the hallways seem so because of their length. The walls are constructed of concrete block that has polished surfaces

The Curtis Meyer House, Galesbury, Mich. (1950)

RIGHT and BELOW
**The Kenneth Laurent
House, Rockford, Ill.
(1949)**

which are more elegant than untreated block. There were custom-made rugs designed by Wright and embellished with small accents of colour.

It is not apparent at first sight, but the 1949 **Howard Anthony House** of Benton Harbor, Michigan is nearly identical in plan to the McCartney house of Parkwyn Village, Kalamazoo. The bedroom wing is longer in the Anthony house because of an extended room at the end which Anthony used as a laboratory. The elevated courtyard is unexpected because it makes snow removal difficult, while the living room overlooks a flood plain and has a fine view.

Slightly south of the Anthony house and looking in the opposite direction into the ravine is the **Carl Schultz House** built several years later in St. Joseph, Michigan in 1957. The house is set back away from the street at the edge of the drop. The living room is very large and has a circular hearth for the fireplace. There is a very large automobile court which makes the house appear even larger.

Looking west from a high bluff on the eastern shore of Lake Michigan, the view from the **Dr. Ina Morris Harper House**, St. Joseph, Michigan (1950) can be spectacular but can be limited as well when snow piles

LEFT
The Charles Weltzheimer House, Oberlin, Ohio (1948)

BELOW
The Albert Adelman House, Fox Point, Wisc. (1948)

The Ina Morris Harper House, St. Joseph, Mich. (1959)

**The Sol Friedman House,
Pleasantville, New York
(1949)**

**The Edward Serlin
House, Pleasantville,
New York (1949)**

investigating their successful implementation. A long bedroom was added to the house to accommodate the growing family. Reisley has written a history of the Pleasantville project and it would be similarly interesting if publications were forthcoming from the participants of the two other developments.

The editor of the famous *Arizona Highways* was Raymond Carlson who had published an article on Wright's work which led to the two becoming acquainted. The **Carlson House** shows evidence of another departure in its construction. The house is based on a 4sq ft (1.2m²) module defined by 4 x 4ft wooden posts with insulated panels used to span the posts. This system works well apart from a few instances where turns and room entrances can be rather tight. The spaces are superior to most other Usonian houses.

Herman T. Mossberg of South Bend, Indiana waited from 1946 until 1948 for the construction of his house. Jack Howe was more involved in the design and construction of the **Mossberg House** than in some of the other Wright designs and it is more subdued as a result, though with a larger, more generous scale than most Usonian houses. The stairway has an extremely modern appearance with its treads held in

position by metal rods inserted between ceiling and floor.

Thomas Keys was fortunate in having Wright realize a design from the late 1930s for his house in Rochester, in 1950. The earth-bermed design was proposed for a cooperative development to be located outside Detroit. The combination of the hipped and flat roofs is unique but adds to the small appearance. The berms help direct the breezes to the windows and through the house as it does in the Jacobs II house.

The **Arthur Mathews House**, Atherton, California is one of the later Usonian houses that wraps around to form a courtyard, the extensions of the roof hips adding to the appearance of enclosure. The street elevation consists of a long brick wall with widely spaced windows with square wooden awnings that appear almost medieval in appearance.

Dr. Alvin Miller of Charles City, Iowa has the only boat slip designed by Wright and is on the Cedar river that runs through Iowa. The stonework is of the finest quality, almost equalling that of Taliesin.

Growing up on the family farm, getting married and raising a family on the same farm, might not afford many opportunities for such a departure from other examples in the locality but **Robert Muirhead**, of Plato Center, Illinois took advantage of his acreage in 1950 and built a very long

The Raymond Carlson House, Phoenix, Ariz. (1950)

**The Robert Muirhead
House, Plato Center, Ill.
(1950)**

**The William Palmer
House, Ann Arbor, Mich.
(1950)**

ABOVE

The Donald Schaberg House, Okemos, Mich. (1950)

ABOVE RIGHT

The Seymour Shavin House, Chattanooga, Tenn. (1950)

RIGHT

The Richard Smith House, Jefferson, Wisc. (1959)

1950 and the Palmers are still adding to them.

The major lumber dealer in the capital of Michigan was **Don Schaberg** who built his Wright design in nearby Okemos in 1950. The house is located on the far east end of town and has several acres with a swimming pool that was added later.

The **Seymour Shavin House**, in Chattanooga, Tennessee, is the only Wright design in the state, where it is located on the east end of a ridge and is much less noticeable than the others on the block, so much so that it is possible to pass it by without noticing it. The living room is at the highest point of the house with the bedroom wing, providing the tranquillity which was a requirement of the client.

The street elevation of the **Richard Smith House**, Jefferson, Wisconsin has no windows to speak of but there are small openings that allow light to penetrate the hall and living room. On the side facing the Meadow Springs Golf Course, however, the living and dining room walls are nearly all glass. These form a court and surround a great oak tree that provides a canopy to the courtyard and the entire house.

As a naval architect and engineer, **J.A. Sweeton** of Cherry Hill, New Jersey could

appreciate the innovations proposed for his modest house and for such a small building there are many of them. A steel beam holds the roof rafters but it is not located at the ridge but rather allows the rafters to cantilever past the beam and meet at the ridge.

David Wright was the fifth child of Wright and his first wife, Catherine, and had worked for the Portland Cement Association in Chicago before deciding to move to Phoenix, Arizona. He thought that someone in the family should make use of his father's

talents and in return received a most unusual design well suited to the desert climate. The house is raised off the ground to avoid the heat and to catch the breezes that run across the top of the orange trees of the orchard where it was built.

The house is actually a wide and long ramp in form, constructed from concrete block that sits atop the concrete ramp, the interior finished with mahogany to offset the cool grey of the block. One of the greatest graphic designs of the Usonian era is featured

ABOVE
The J.A. Sweeton House, Cherry Hill, N.J. (1959)

ABOVE LEFT
The David Wright House, Phoenix, Ariz. (1950)

The Robert Berger House, San Anselmo, Calif. (1950)

time and building talent. Berger received his design and took a night job so that he could build his house himself during daylight hours.

The father of Albert and the owner of a successful laundry in Milwaukee, **Ben Adelman** commissioned a winter house for Phoenix, Arizona. This building was constructed using inexpensive native labour and utilizes what Wright called his Usonian Automatic System. The concrete blocks were

large and made from local materials often found on the site and similar to those used at the Arizona Biltmore, located just across the back yard from the house.

Two sisters, **Gabrielle & Charlcy Austin**, born in Greenville, South Carolina, wrote to Wright before 1951 concerning a house for themselves. Both were spinsters and librarians. The sisters did not live in the house for long and lived in much more

conventional houses both before and after their Wright design. The house is located on the edge of a shallow ravine that has few other houses bordering it.

The 1951 **A. K. Chahroudi Cottage**, Mahopac, New York is built on a small 10-acre (4-hectare) island in a lake just north of New York City and was to be the first of at least two buildings on the island. The other was to be a large house with deep curved

The Benjamin Adelman House, Phoenix, Ariz. (1951)

Before a major addition and remodelling

The Gabrielle & Charlcy Austin House, Greenville, S.C. (1951)

cantilevers that reached out over the surface of the lake. According to new ordinances, the house could not be built that way but the current owner still has it in mind to try.

The pointed pitched roofs of the **S.P. Elam** house in Austin, Minnesota exaggerates the length of the roof cantilevers. The stonework in the house is some of the best and can be favourably compared to that of Taliesin. The living room is almost an afterthought in its location and proportions, perhaps as a result of difficulties which arose between architect and client.

The roof size of the **Charles F. Glore House**, Lake Forest, Illinois might lead one to believe that this is a large house; but in fact the rooms are small. The dining room is a 9 x 9ft (2.7 x 2.7m) alcove off the main hall and the site is large and beautifully landscaped. However, the house has had a difficult history with many owners, one for almost every three years of its existence.

John Haynes of Fort Wayne, Indiana built his Wright house in 1951 on a very tight budget, as was the case with the majority of post-war clients. As with most of them, the Haynes family outgrew the house

**The A.K. Chahroudi
Cottage, Lake Mahopac,
New York (1951)**

OPPOSITE
The S.P. Elam House, Austin, Minn. (1951)

LEFT
The Herbert F. Glore House, Lake Forest, Ill. (1951)

after a relatively short time but unlike most of the others, Haynes built a house to the south next door, which was not designed by Wright.

There are few other examples of small towns possessing a cluster of Wright-designed buildings but Canton, Ohio is not one of them. The town is within range of Pittsburgh and Cleveland with middle-class inhabitants. Nathan Rubin and Ellis Feiman are related through family and were acquainted with John Dobkins. **The Rubin**

LEFT
The John Haynes House, Fort Wayne, Ind. (1951)

The Andrew B. Cooke House, Virginia Beach, Virginia (1952)

but in the direction of an inland waterway, being more protected in this location from the occasional hurricanes that destroy most of the coastal houses. The living room forms a large arc with the water as its focus.

Wright was always eager to accommodate his clients' requirements and the 1953 design for **Louis Penfield** in Willoughby was no exception. Penfield was as tall as most normal doors, 6ft 8in (2m), and Wright's response was to raise the ceiling heights in otherwise low areas to a more comfortable 8ft (2.4m). The property was large and bordered the Chagrin river. Penfield had a second house designed and his son is now intending to build it on the same piece of land.

LEFT

The Toufic Kalil House, Manchester, N.H. (1955)

BELOW LEFT

The Louis Penfield House, Willoughby Hills, Ohio (1953)

BELOW

The Frank Sander House, Stamford, Conn. (1953)

RIGHT

The Robert Llewellyn Wright House, Bethesda, Maryland (1953)

OPPOSITE

The Jorgine Boomer House, Phoenix, Ariz. (1953)

Although the Sturges house is at the other end of the continent from the **Frank Sander House** in Stamford, Connecticut, the two houses are very similar in plan though not in effect – neither do they have similar views. The Sander site is not as steep, making it more accommodating to its residents. The cantilevered porches were not as well suited for the north-east as the south-west and were therefore enclosed in glass.

Jorgine Boomer had come from New York City where her husband had managed the Waldorf Astoria Hotel. Her initial idea was to purchase the burned-out ruins of the Pauson house in Phoenix, Arizona. However, she did not buy it but instead formed a partnership with Mrs Pauson to purchase land surrounding the ruins. On one of the lots, she had Wright design a tiny house with large windows framing views of the nearby mountains which, despite its size, still

RIGHT
The E. Clarke Arnold House, Columbus, Wisc. (1954)

OPPOSITE TOP LEFT
The Abraham Wilson House, Millstone, N.J. (1954)

OPPOSITE TOP RIGHT, BOTTOM LEFT and RIGHT
The John E. Christian House, West Lafayette, Ind. (1954)

allowed for a chauffeur's quarters.

Frank Lloyd Wright's youngest son from his first marriage, **Robert L. Wright**, was an attorney in Bethesda, Maryland, which is a suburb of Washington, D.C. He decided to follow his older brother David's lead and have his father design him a house. Robert was quite a sports fan which may account for the inspiration of the plan shape, which is a football. The house is constructed from concrete block and mahogany and overlooks a thicket of tall trees and bushes. Some of the furniture his father designed repeats the sporting theme.

The **E. Clarke Arnold House** in Columbus, Wisconsin is similar in many ways to the nearby Smith house of Jefferson. Here again, the street side is almost windowless while the rear is nearly all windows. It is also set on a parallelogram which opens the angle between the wings much more than an ordinary 90° rectangular plan.

Wright took the available square footage and crammed most of the rooms into the smallest area in the **Abraham Wilson House**, Millstone, New Jersey. This allowed for the largest living room possible which is, on a practical level, a full two storeys; but because the second floor is so low, it does not tower over the room. This excess is required because of the gardens which it overlooks.

John E. Christian is one of the pioneers of nuclear biology, having invented the system in which radioactive drugs can be traced through an animal's biological system. He was a professor at Purdue University in

The Maurice Greenberg House, Dousman, Wisc. (1954)

Indiana and he and his wife spent several years in consultation with Wright concerning the design of their house. Once the house was under way in 1954, it would be another 40 years before everything was finished to their high specifications, the last item to be put in place being the elaborate copper fascia. This is one of the finest of Wright's Usonian designs and the house has been placed in trust to ensure its future. Moreover, an extensive educational programme is being developed with the buildings as its focus.

The **Dr. Maurice Greenberg House** is probably the closest in concept to the Kaufmann house, Fallingwater, than any other. The house is built on the brow of a hill in the same manner as Taliesin and, like the Christian house, there is still work to be completed. Even now, Dr. Greenberg has a store of bricks under tarpaulin.

Isaac N. Hagan of Chalk Hill, Pennsylvania ran the family dairy and ice cream business in a small town just south of Fallingwater. Where Fallingwater is flamboyant, however, the Hagan house of 1954 is restrained. The Hagans sold it several years ago and the new owner has now opened it to the public.

William Thaxton wished to build a development of Wright houses on the west side of Houston, Texas, being himself involved in real estate and insurance. He built a house that he moved into himself

The Isaac Newton Hagan House, Ohiopyle, Penn. (1954)

is the **Dr. Robert Walton House** in Modesto which, though designed in 1957, was not built until 1961. The house has a full set of Wright-designed furniture that was built by the finish carpenter for the house. It is one of Wright's longest houses and has five bedrooms.

The **Allen Friedman House** in Bannockburn, Illinois was designed in 1956, but was probably one of the last to be constructed while Wright was still

**The Conrad E. Gordon
House, Wilsonville,
Oregon (1957)**

**The Donald Lovness
House, Stillwater, Minn.
(1955)**

advice in an area in which he was becoming
expert, prefabrication. Erdman had been
designing and building small-town medical
buildings and launched the Erdman Prefabs
at a house builder's convention in Chicago.
There were several built in his home town of
Madison and as far away as New York City.

There were two basic designs – a low
gabled house and a compact two-storey flat-
roofed design. The project was not an
overwhelming success as only nine of the first

houses were built and just two of the taller,
flat-roofed units. These include the **Eugene
Van Tamlen House** in Madison, Wisconsin,
the **Al Borah** in Barrington, Illinois, the
Donald Duncan in Lisle, Illinois, the **Arnold
Jackson** near Madison, the **Frank Iber** north
of Milwaukee, and the **Socrates Zaferiou** on
the Hudson river north of New York.

The two Erdman Prefab #2s are the
Walter Rudin, also in Madison, and the
James McBean in Rochester, Minnesota. All

Arizona, which were finished by the architects he left behind in his firm and it was not until 1967 that the house construction was completed for Lykes. Naturally, there is some controversy as to whether this building should be considered a Frank Lloyd Wright design; but since it was for the same site and the same client, it appears that it could be so regarded. The last of Wright's designs is based on a circle and his first, the Winslow house, was based on the square. Between the two there were over 1,000 designs and over 500 buildings.

During an interview, Wright was asked why he had designed so many houses during his long career. His response was, 'Because they ask me for them.' In taking the broad view of Wright's career, it does not appear

The George Ablin House, Bakersfield, Calif. (1958)

The Donald Stromquist House. Bountiful, Utah (1958)

and real definitions towards which he could work.

As 'ordinary' or common as some of Wright's solutions may have become, all of his work is generally superior to that of others of his calling. The quality of the space and the ability of the light to form the space is both uncommon and rare. There are few opportunities now to experience what Wright left behind as there are fewer than 400 houses in total and more and more of them are being turned into museums or taken out of circulation.

RIGHT
The Paul Olfelt House, St. Louis Park, Minn. (1958)

that he ever ignored Henry Hobson Richardson's first three laws of architecture: Get the job, get the job and finally, get the job. Wright took on a wide range of large and amazingly small design projects, even at the height of his career and popularity. No job seemed to be too great or too insignificant: if one persisted, one could get him to do just about anything. We have seen remodellings and garages as well as interiors large and small. These were for long-term clients as well as complete strangers. Wright had an overriding need to create and when there were no clients he was at his lowest ebb. He was unable to spirit a design out of thin air; he always needed a real site

The Seth Peterson Cottage, Lake Delton, Wisc. (1958)

The Duey Wright House, Wasau, Wisc. (1958)

**The Norman Lykes
House, Phoenix, Ariz.
(1966)**

BELOW and RIGHT
**The Romeo and Juliet
Windmill, Spring Green,
Wisc. (1896)**
Hillside II (to the left) and
Hillside I (to the right) are in
the foreground

Frank Lloyd Wright's
Studio, Oak Park, Ill.
(1897)

would embrace him, while together they would withstand all that nature could throw at them. At the time, his uncles were quoted as remarking that it would blow down in the first strong wind; however, to their amazement, it still stands today, well over a

100 years later when almost everything his other relatives built, no matter how well, is long since gone.

In contrast to the picturesque profile of Wright's 1889 house on Forest Avenue, his own architectural **Studio, Oak Park**, 1897,

stands on Chicago Avenue on the same property. It faces the busy commercial street and is a complex amalgamation of different parts, each function clearly defined in its exterior. The tall octagonal library to the west housed paperwork as well as his drawings,

OPPOSITE and LEFT
**The Hillside Home
School, Spring Green,
Wisc. (1902)**
Shown after the addition
and conversion by Wright to
include facilities for the
Taliesin Fellowship in 1932
and after

and also served as a conference room for client meetings, there being no windows at eye level to distract from the matters in hand. The book-lined walls were designed to act as an acoustical insulation against the street noise, as well as the sound of conversation in the library.

The entrance led into the reception room where visitors would be directed. A large plan table was in evidence with a source of light coming from above as well as from the north where prospective contractors were discussed in preparation for their bids. Behind the reception room was Wright's office – also used by his secretary to keep the accounts – and there was a typewriter for correspondence and the preparation of specifications.

The largest feature was the two-storey drafting room on the east end of the structure which was square on its first floor and had an octagonal balcony above. The centre of the second level was open, admitting light to the drafting areas.

Throughout the Studio, there were three fireplaces: one in the library, and a single chimney serving the two in the drafting room and the office. This was not the only source of heat as the outside walls had large radiators – it would have been difficult for a draftsman to operate efficiently with cold fingers.

The Studio was connected directly to Wright's house through the original dining room. A pitched-ceilinged hallway was created and built around and incorporated a living willow tree that was on no account to be sacrificed during the construction. This building served Wright until he left for Europe in 1909 though he remodelled the studio in 1911 upon his return for use as a residential property that would bring in an income for the family he left behind. After his divorce from Catherine, it was sold in 1924.

Wright's aunts, Nell and Jane, were good women and equally good exponents of their craft and their school was filled to capacity in a very short time. Again, they turned to their nephew for a new and much larger building, which took the form, in 1902, of **Hillside Home School** in the Jones Valley. In a manner reminiscent of his Oak Park Studio but more modern in appearance, like the Susan Lawrence Dana House of Springfield, the school building was a composition of

several parts and there were actually two buildings connected by a bridge over the new driveway. The main building, that which faced the road, had the individual classrooms lined up on two floors connecting the gymnasium and the assembly hall with its kitchen below. Across the bridge was the science laboratory and the drawing studio. The science laboratory was named after Susan Dana because of her generous gift of the room and a large cash donation to the school, and was built by Wright's uncle Thomas. The stone base consisted of local light-brown limestone with rows of diamond-paned windows above.

Wright bought this and other school buildings from his aunts many years later and turned it to his own use for his school of architecture, the Taliesin Fellowship. He added a very large, truss-roofed drafting room directly to the north of the science and art rooms, while to the east and west sides were smaller dormitory rooms for the students that are in use today.

The final design for the **Abraham Lincoln Center** of Chicago may not have been completely attributable to Wright although he took credit for most of it in an article published in 1900. Jenkin Lloyd Jones, Wright's uncle, commissioned the building and the two appear to have been very close indeed. It is situated at the north-east corner of the intersection of Langley and Oakwood

and across the street to the south from the first church built in Chicago for Jones. All Souls Church was designed by Silsbee, who had been Wright's first employer over 20 years earlier. While the Silsbee building resembled a shingled house, the Lincoln Center is a tall brick building of six storeys.

Jones was most impressed by Abraham Lincoln and there is a note in the Jones family records to the effect that Jenkin's nephew Frank's middle name was Lincoln long before it was Lloyd, though this may or may not be true. For many years he wrote his name as Frank L. Wright, but on his marriage certificate, the ceremony having been performed by Jones, it is given as Lloyd.

Wright had never before designed a building as large or as complicated as the Lincoln Center, and decided to form a partnership with one of his friends from Steinway Hall, Dwight H. Perkins, who had been in practice in Chicago. Perkins had already designed large buildings, including Steinway Hall where Wright and his contemporaries had had their offices, and which was owned by Wright's first client, William Winslow and his brother.

The building was designed to serve the needs of the growing congregation and a large auditorium with several smaller gathering rooms were included, along with many offices and classrooms. Throughout the interior are details which accurately reflect

The Abraham Lincoln Center, Chicago, Ill. (1903)

**The Horse Show
Association Fountain,
Oak Park, Ill. (1903)**

Wright's thinking at the time, for example, the headline trim and quarter-sawn oak spindles.

Wright's involvement in the design of the **Horse Show Fountain** of 1903 was at the suggestion of Richard Bock who was a sculptor that Wright had worked with on several earlier projects. Bock was the designer of the fountain, with suggestions coming from Wright; however, it no longer exists in its original form having been moved to a corner from the centre of the block, its original location. It was a common drinking fountain, accommodating dogs as well as horses at its lower basins.

One of the finest and most integrated of all Wright's designs was the 1903 **Larkin Company Administration Building** in Buffalo, and Wright brought all of his architectural abilities to bear on this five-storey structure, which was innovative in its scale and in every system – structural, electrical, mechanical and visual. Wright devised what may be the first air conditioning system that incorporated refrigeration and air cleansing through a spray of water. Heat was provided by radiation and the large skylight was supplemented by incandescent lighting. The intercom system was innovative as well but too little is known concerning its use and design to determine the full extent of its ingenuity. The building had elevators as well as stairways and the stairs were in the tall

corner piers in the same locations as those of the Unity Temple.

It appears that John Larkin had originally been seeking to use the Adler & Sullivan office for the design of his building.

Unfortunately, Adler had abandoned architecture and Sullivan was now operating on his own and not doing as well as one might have expected.

Wright's initial drawings bore some

The Larkin Company Administration Building, Buffalo, New York (1903)

ABOVE

The E-Z Polish Company, Chicago, III. (1905)

ABOVE RIGHT

The River Forest Tennis Club, III. (1906)

resemblance to products coming from the Adler & Sullivan office, and Wright may have been made previously aware of Larkin's interest. As it turned out, the mass of the building changed little through all its development until it reached its final form.

Two brothers operated the **E-Z Polish Company** and owned the factory in Chicago built about 1905, following the completion of the Darwin D. Martin House in Buffalo, New York for one of the two Martin brothers. The other partner and brother was William E. Martin, also a Wright client but from nearby

Oak Park, and it was William who introduced his brother Darwin to Wright. The E-Z Polish Company was a part of the Martin & Martin Company and made stove polish among other products. The utilitarian nature of the brick belies the simplicity and elegance of the proportions of the building, though the planning is at the same high level of quality as the Larkin building. The stairs are set at the ends, allowing full use of each floor space. The building consists of a concrete frame with the Chicago common brick used as fireproof infill material that was

very inexpensive. Wright even designed the orange-and-black graphics and typeface for the company letterhead.

The **River Forest Tennis Club** was originally located north of the busy intersection of Harlem and Quick, just north of Lake Street at the border that separates Oak Park from River Forest. It was built in 1906 for less then $3,000 but the building was cut into three pieces and pulled by horses to its new and current site in about 1920. Since its relocation there have been several alterations and additions.

The date assigned to the remodelling of the lobby of the **Rookery Building** in Chicago is one of the most enigmatic. The detailing appears to be a throwback to the pre-1900 era, as does the elaborate gold leaf used throughout which may have been at the request of the client. This building was owned by Edward C. Waller, a Wright client and neighbour of William Winslow in River Forest. The Rookery Building was designed by Burnham & Root in what was and remains one of the premier office locations in Chicago, situated in the heart of the financial district. Before the era of electricity, gas lights were used and because the light emitted was not strong enough, rooms could not be deep and daylight could not penetrate far unless the ceilings were high. The glass-covered court allowed light into the interior and presented an excellent opportunity for the original architects to include a spectacular circular staircase on the west wall of the lightcourt which pierces the glass-ceilinged lobby.

The Rookery Building, Chicago, Ill. (1905)

291

RIGHT
**The Rookery Building
Lobby, Chicago, Ill. (1905)**

OPPOSITE
**The Smith Bank, Dwight,
Ill. (1905)**

It was in this central lobby that Wright's design was to be found. It connected to the LaSalle Street main entrance and the Adams Street side as well, and to transmit more light to the space, the floor of the surrounding balcony was constructed of glass panels set into small, square metal frames. This may have been one of the first uses of this device manufactured by the Luxfer Prism Company.

Frank L. Smith played a good game of baseball and at one time came up against Ty Cobb and his New York Yankees when they arrived in Dwight at a railroad stopover on the Illinois Central line that runs through it, and is the *raison d'être* for the town. Smith was in real estate and decided he needed a way to assist his clients in financing their purchases as well as making money for himself. So he founded a bank and Wright developed a storefront design that consisted of a 60ft (18.3m) façade. What is unusual about this is the inclusion of a fireplace to be used in an office. The building as seen today consists of a single interior space, but when Wright designed it, one side was for Smith's real-estate office and the other for banking operations. There was a full set of furniture designed by Wright for both, though most of it has been sold off over the years. One of Smith's partners, R.S. Ludington, was also a client of Wright's and commissioned a house design which was

never built. Ludington later moved to central Washington and was involved in hiring Wright for a design of a part of the Wenatchee Bank, Dwight, Illinois in 1905.

Dr. W.H. Pettit spent most of his life running his practice in Iowa. His brother-in-law was William A. Glasner, whose own Wright house, built by a ravine in Glencoe, was just about finished. After Pettit died in 1905, his wife commissioned Wright not only for a memorial headstone but for something that would also be of benefit to the entire community for many years to come. The **Pettit Memorial Chapel** of Belvidere, Illinois was built in the Belvidere cemetery on the family plot.

Unity Temple, Oak Park, is one of the masterpieces of Wright's career and the complete integration of all systems, structural, visual, mechanical, electrical and plumbing are masterfully executed, an example being the large columns that hold up the roof of the main temple which are hollow and act as air ducts for the room. The vents are highlighted with the application of oak trim which continues around the room and identifies other significant visual devices invented by Wright.

The design of the Unity Temple may be based on a temple Wright saw on his 1905 trip to Japan which had two parts, one for religious operations and the other for secular activities, and has its parallel in the temple

Unity Temple, Oak Park, Ill. (1906)

ABOVE
A rare archive photograph of the Unity Temple under construction

RIGHT
Interior view of the podium

room and social hall on opposite sides of the central entry.

The temple room has two balconies on each of the three sides and stairways in all four corners. There is a full skylight in the temple auditorium and several more in the social room. There are windows at the top of the four walls and they form a continuous line.

Perhaps the most important feature of Unity Temple is that it is one of the first non-industrial buildings to be constructed using poured concrete. Previously, concrete had been used for fire-proof storage and manufacturing, as in the E-Z Polish building.

Unity Temple, Oak Park, Ill. (1906)

Interior of the social room on the opposite side of the entry from the temple room

Unity Temple, Oak Park, Ill. (1906)

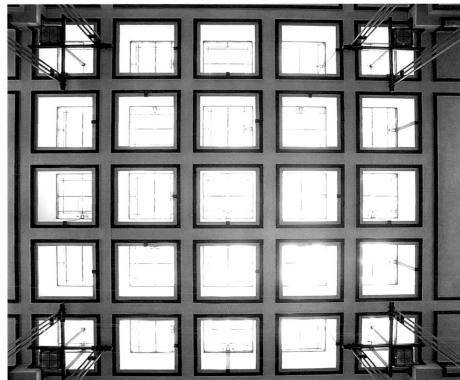

When the use of the material in this concept was observed, many, especially in Europe, where concrete was more widely used, took particular note. This was indeed a bold move, using an inexpensive material to create such an artful form.

Charles E. Roberts, a Wright client but unrelated to Isabel Roberts, one of Wright's employees, used his powers of persuasion on the Unity Temple building committee on Wright's behalf and supported Wright in his work and personal life over many years.

The commission for the 1909 **City National Bank** in Mason City came about

Unity Temple, Oak Park, Ill. (1906)

ABOVE
Looking up at the temple ceiling

ABOVE LEFT
Interior of the temple room from the upper balcony

LEFT
The entry to the space between the temple room on the left and the social room on the right

City National Bank and Hotel, Mason City, Iowa (1909)

when the father of a student attending Wright's aunts' Hillside Home School was impressed with its design and spoke to the staff concerning Wright's methods. For a small prairie town like Mason City, there was already a high ratio of good design present. Mason City has a river, the Winnebago, running through it and is sometimes referred to as 'River City'. If this sounds familiar it is because it was the location of a musical called *The Music Man*, and a few of the scenes in the movie starring Robert Preston and Shirley Jones were set there, though none of the Wright buildings or other Prairie designs are featured.

There were two buildings which were part of the same project, the bank and the hotel. The main banking room was tall, about one-and-a-half storeys high, and there was a wonderful arched door to the vaults and several bronze figures modelled by Richard Bock situated above the tellers. Many years earlier, the bank had been remodelled and raised in height by a few feet. The former bank room also held retail establishments. The hotel was still in use into the 1970s but was eventually converted into offices.

Each building can be taken as a separate entity because, although they had a common wall, they were not interconnected. The bank was built of a substantial brick and the hotel was originally stucco. The bank also had what is called tapestry brick, which consisted of coloured brick interspersed with light tan.

Midway Gardens was intended as a concert venue but became a beer garden later on. The client was Edward C. Waller Jr., whose father was responsible for the remodelling of the River Forest house and the Rookery lobby project. The site of Midway Gardens had been a centre of entertainment long before the new construction was envisaged, and was at the west end of what was the Midway Pleasance dating from the Columbian Exposition and World Fair of 1893. Wright developed several schemes of differing sizes and orientations before deciding on the definitive one. The

construction period was limited and had to be finished on time because a famous conductor and celebrated singers were scheduled for the inauguration. The story goes that the paint was still not dry as the

guests were entering the Gardens on opening night.

Although the venture was a success, it was unable to carry the increasing burden of debt. Waller lost the property following which

301

RIGHT and OPPOSITE
The Albert D. German Warehouse, Richland Center, Wisc. (1915)

style and to reinterpret it using a more modern vocabulary, without resorting to the outright imitation that so many classical architects engaged in on a regular basis.

Probably the largest and most complex project of Wright's career was the **Imperial Hotel**, Tokyo, Japan of 1916–1922. It was composed of and built in several sections, and it was these very sections, and their ability to move independently of one another while connected but not attached, that allowed the building to survive the worst earthquake of Japan's history in 1923.

Wright first became fascinated in the late 1880s with Japan and things Japanese through his former employer, Joseph Lyman Silsbee, who had been one of the earliest collectors of Japanese wood-block prints. This was at a time when Japan was just opening up to trade, and the sudden exposure of Japanese culture to the Western world was powerful and unexpected. It influenced many artists of the time, including James McNeill Whistler and Claude Monet, and inspired a book on Japanese architecture by the American Ralph Adams Cram which has been of interest to many practitioners of architecture over several decades.

Wright saw Japanese artefacts for himself at the 1893 Columbian Exhibition and World's Fair, held in Chicago at a time when he was preparing to leave the firm of Adler & Sullivan, and it is thought that he and

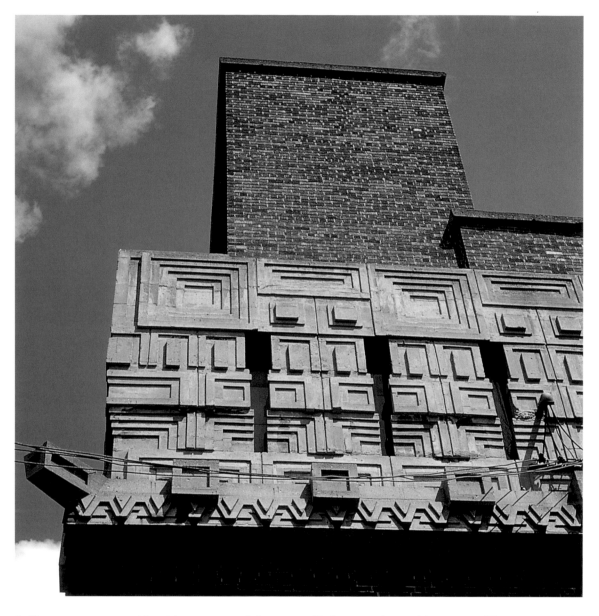

Sullivan spent a considerable amount of time viewing and analyzing these exhibits. Wright began to collect Japanese wood-block prints himself and became one of the most important dealers and collectors of the genre.

Unfortunately, and because of his occasional financial problems, he was forced to sell parts of the collection; but he did loan out some of the best work for at least two exhibitions at the Art Institute of Chicago in

LEFT and OPPOSITE
**The Imperial Hotel,
Tokyo, Japan (1916–1922)**
Interior detail of
reconstruction

311

RIGHT and OPPOSITE
**The Johnson Wax
Administration Building,
Racine, Wisc. (1936)**

RIGHT
The Kansas City Community Christian Church, Kansas City, Missouri (1940)

OPPOSITE
The Soloman R. Guggenheim Museum, New York City (1943–59)

The project went through several evolutions over the 16 years the museum was waiting to be built. The first 1943 scheme had the basic components already in place. It showed a right-hand blue hexagonal tower framed by ivory pieces which was balanced by an office suite at the left-hand side. The second scheme had the tapered circular tower on the right but the colour had been changed to red. The tower was tapered from bottom to top, the reverse of its current design. The third development reversed the tower taper but was first shown as a seven-level and then as a five- before the final four-level tower was completed. Before it was finished, Wright tried the tower on the left.

Wright intended the works of art to be featured in a setting unusual for a picture gallery. The paintings, executed on ordinary canvas, were to be shown as they had been painted, on easels set within the downward spiralling ramp. The niches between the columns were intended for sculpture with the walls of the niches pitched outward at the top and curving along their length as they descended the spiral. The wall was neither flat nor square and not a very good fit for a rectangular work of art, a factor which has been largely ignored when hanging the museum's exhibits. The indentations of the tower were intended to gently illuminate the exhibits with natural daylight; unfortunately, they have been

enclosed and filled with fluorescent lights.

The pathway as originally envisaged by Wright was much less steep, as the visitor was taken to the top of the ramp by the small elevator and was then meant to proceed in a serpentine direction past the easels and into the niches all the way down to the main floor. According to some visitors, the act of viewing the exhibits can be a slightly disorientating experience.

Soloman R. Guggenheim Museum, New York City (1943–59)
RIGHT
View from the gallery

OPPOSITE
Detail of glass dome

As with most of Wright's religious buildings, the 1947 **Unitarian Church** in Shorewood Hills had a very small budget and it was necessary to search far and wide for a contractor who could balance Wright's stringent specifications with the finance allowed. By chance, there was such a person right in Madison, and doing a good line of business. He had graduated from the University of Illinois at Urbana with a degree in architecture and had always admired Wright's work. Marshall Erdman decided to take the job on this basis, although he expected to lose money on the project. However, he also expected to gain more from the the experience than he would lose.

The building has several important design innovations. Starting at the bottom, there are no foundations. The building is constructed upon a 9-inch (23-cm) deep base of 3-inch (7.6-cm) gravel, non-graded. Above it is a 9 inch grade beam that takes the loads and distributes it to the ground.

At the other end, the roof is constructed with a series of trusses which are tapered from the centre to both ends. Plaster is applied to the interior while a sheet copper roof with repeating patterns covers the building with wide overhangs.

The benches were made of standard fir plywood, the design being a simple one in the form of a deep seat supported by two plywood legs. The back was hinged to

RIGHT and OPPOSITE
**The Meeting House of
the Unitarian Church,
Shorewood Hills, Wisc.
(1947)**

another piece of plywood about the same size at the seat and was held in place with short sections of chain. However, these benches have been replaced in the 50 years or more since the building's completion.

One of the finest compositions of Wright's career was the **V.C. Morris Gift Shop** in San Francisco in which Wright managed to make a simple wall of brick masonry into a work of art. It was as sophisticated as any of the best graphic design and transforms itself from day to night with its innovative lighting scheme. The entrance is a tapered glass cave and, once inside, one is surprised at the gently curved ramp which is reminiscent of the Guggenheim Museum.

Along the walls of the ramp were circular niches for the display of the fine items Morris' always had in stock. The interior was a remodelling of a typical warehouse and the old warehouse can still be seen between the circular light fixtures on the ceiling.

The 1950 **First Christian Church** in Phoenix was originally designed for the

ABOVE and RIGHT
The V.C. Morris Gift Shop,
San Francisco, Calif.
(1948)

South-West Christian Seminary for another site, also in Phoenix. The congregation approached Mrs Wright in 1966 and asked her for permission to start the building, which was not begun until 1973, the 122-ft (37-m) bell tower being finished in 1978.

The **Anderton Court** shopping precinct in Beverly Hills does not have the exposed areas that one might expect in an open-air market with retail stores on several levels. The tower adds to the verticality of the design in what would otherwise be a standard row of shops and is also the centre of the stairway that connects all of the levels with one another. The complex is one of the most expensive retail outlets in the United States. The simple stucco surfaces, however, are in several cases obscured by the gaudily-lit shop signs, but the multi-level design makes the most of the space available. There are three levels in some parts of the building and a few of the shops are below grade.

Wright first developed the concept for the 1952 **Price Tower** around 1929 for a tiny site for St. Mark's-in-the-Bowerie, in New York City. It is said that the design of the

The First Christian Church, Phoenix, Ariz. (1950)

tower came about because Price, having made a good living, wished to give something back to the community. Along with his sons, he decided to call on Wright to commission a three-storey building with 25,000sq ft (2250m²) of floor space. Wright's opinion was that three storeys were inefficient and suggested ten floors instead. In the end they finally agreed on a 19-storey

office and apartment building and Price was proud of the resulting creation he and Wright had produced together.

The building is constructed much like a tree. It has a sturdy, thick trunk with the elevators for the apartments and the offices located along it, as well as the electrical and plumbing conduits and pipes. Wright referred to it as the tree that had escaped the forest.

It was erected in a small town in a neighbourhood with one- or two-storey houses and no other tall buildings; the 19-storey building must therefore have been plainly visible for many miles.

The tower is divided into four quadrants. Three are for offices and one for a duplex apartment which takes up part of two floors, the upper floor containing two

RIGHT and OPPOSITE
**The Beth Sholom
Synagogue, Elkins Park,
Penn. (1954)**

brought into the project as one who liked to provide a creative solution for a difficult site and a tight budget and the group was well pleased with the result. The State of Texas did not require Wright to be a registered architect for this project.

The theatre is only 12 rows deep and seats over 400 people. The stage is circular and is able to rise as well as rotate. The site is within the flood plain of Turtle Creek which runs through a park all the way into downtown Dallas and is in one of the best areas of the city.

The **Annunciation Greek Orthodox Church** in Wauwatosa is another of the large religious buildings designed by Wright in the last decade of his life. Again, it is not a formulaic building, following on the successes of his earlier work, and is as unique and original as the Beth Sholom Synagogue. The design won an award from the Portland Cement Association for the innovative method Wright used to support the dome which rests at its edges on small

OPPOSITE

The Kundert Medical Clinic, San Luis Obispo, Calif. (1956)

LEFT

Kenneth L. Meyers Medical Clinic, Dayton, Ohio (1956)

and is at the north end of the campus, just east of the stadium of Wichita State University. It is now used as offices.

A rather more modest project is the 1957 **Fasbender Clinic** in Hastings, Minnesota, and demonstrates how completely at home Wright was with a project of whatever proportions, ever eager to grasp the chance of providing the best solution to any problem which came his way.

As part of a model town in 1938, Wright included, among other building types, a gasoline station. It was innovative in that the cars were serviced by an overhead cantilever from which the filling hoses were suspended.

It was not until 20 years later, in 1957, that he was able to put this idea into practice at the **Lindholm Service Station** in Cloquet. This is a very small building at the busiest intersection of this very small town. The main portion of the building is a simple concrete block structure with several service bays, the cantilevered roof protruding from a two-storey section. However, current laws do not permit service hoses to drop from above and there are now standard pumps in use.

There was a very small but interesting one-storey school building for a site west of the Jones Valley, between two local landmarks, the House-on-the-Rock and

ABOVE
The Lindholm Service Station, Cloquet, Minn. (1957)

RIGHT
The Wyoming Valley School, Spring Green, Wisc. (1957)

The Marin County Civic Center, San Rafael, Calif. (1957–66)

OPPOSITE

The Marin County Civic Center, San Rafael, Calif. (1957–66)

LEFT

The Lockridge Medical Clinic, Whitefish, Montana (1958)

Taliesin's Hillside Home School building. The **Wyoming Valley School** of 1957 was built using standard concrete blocks and is far from being a throwback to the little one-room schoolhouse.

The largest of all of Wright's buildings is the 1957 **Marin County Civic Center** in San Rafael, which is located across from the

Golden Gate Bridge, north of San Francisco. Wright's solution for a difficult site, which was very hilly, was an economical one. Because the cost of flattening a site and moving all the earth would have been too expensive, Wright drew on history and developed a building that responded to the terrain in much the same way as the aqueducts built by the Romans

2,000 years ago and who had the same problem with uneven profiles. As a result, the requirement for rooms of varying sizes fits very well into the variations of floor space on each level.

The building is in two parts with a circular element at the juncture between each part. The circular room houses the county

The Pilgrim Church, Redding, Calif. (1958)

library which opens out to a grass terrace. Through the centre of each wing is a multi-level area surrounded by corridor space, while above is a skylight that provides natural light throughout the day.

Wright also designed a post office and an exhibition pavilion was built on opposite sides of a beautiful lagoon. The drawings

were completed before Wright's death in 1959 and the construction was completed in 1969 in several phases.

The 1958 **Lockridge Medical Clinic** at Whitefish, Montana is one of the most remote of all Wright's buildings. It is a small one-storey brick structure with several roof heights. It was later converted to offices and

is now occupied by the First State Bank.

The **Pilgrim Congregational Church**, Redding, California, 1958 was planned as a building that could be constructed in several parts with the auditorium or sanctuary the first to be completed. At first glance, it looks as if the structural frames that surmount the building are regular bents. Actually, they are

set at an angle and Wright called this his 'boulder Gothic'. The building is set near the top of a small hill at the west side of town and is oriented on a line with the local landmark, Mount Shasta which, though 60 miles (100km) away, is by far the most prominent feature around.

Wright designed but did not oversee the construction of the **Grady Gammage Auditorium**, which fell to Wes Peters after Wright's death. The auditorium's acoustics are famous for their high quality, the Grand Tier being detached from the back wall which releases the sound energy which would otherwise be trapped under the balcony.

Many of the buildings discussed here are familiar, not only to those who see them every day, but are also of special significance in the cities in which they are located. Given Wright's vast output of private houses, many tend to forget the public buildings, some of which are indisputably masterpieces such as the Unity Temple, Johnson Wax and the Guggenheim Museum in New York.

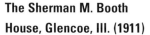

The Sherman M. Booth House, Glencoe, Ill. (1911)

Sherman Booth, the attorney, bought a large piece of land initially intended for a large suburban estate in a prosperous area near Lake Michigan, north of Chicago. Booth handled many things for Wright which included collecting the money owed for the many subscriptions Wright had set up with several architects and others for the purchase of the Wasmuth portfolio. It is likely that Booth became acquainted with Wright through his sister, a Wright client from 1911.

For some reason, Booth did not build this project and scaled back on his own house, ultimately remodelling some smaller buildings nearby the original site. This building took Wright far beyond what he had attempted in his Prairie years. There were large stucco surfaces with no windows and the roofs were no longer low pitched with wide eaves.

The National Life Insurance Company, Chicago, Ill. (1924)

Had this 30-storey building been built, it is entirely possible that Wright's career would have taken a very different direction. The design is an efficient and modern skyscraper which was to have alternating copper and glass panels. The copper was to have been treated with a wash to encourage the development of verdigris, in much the same manner as the Price Tower of the 1950s.

To overcome the problem of lighting, the plan of the building had four projections to the south allowing light to be admitted across the entire floors of the offices.

There were four sets of elevators, one servicing each of the projections and thus distributing the load that occurs at the start and end of each working day. In diagrams, Wright plotted the evacuation of the building on a minute by minute basis, demonstrating the method by which an even flow could be achieved.

The Daphne Funeral Home, San Francisco, Calif. (1945)

Nicholas Daphne interviewed several well known and well-respected architects before building his modern funeral home at the top of one of the high points in that hilly city. The site has wonderful views and lies just west of the San Francisco Mint, one of the oldest in the United States.

Wright produced impressions of two buildings, one a rectangular scheme for offices and flower shops, and the other, that was to contain the chapels, in a circular mode. Underground were other facilities intended for storage and preparation.

Daphne provided several lists of requirements which were helpful in the design and layout of the property. However, Wright was ultimately unable to satisfy Daphne and he sought another architect, Quincy Jones, for the execution of the building.

PACIFIC DWELLINGS FOR MR AND MR
SAN FRANCISCO
FRANK LLOYD WRIGHT ARCHITECT

The V.C. Morris House (Seacliff), San Francisco, Calif. (1945)

Morris was apparently so well pleased with the plan Wright had devised for his gift shop that he commissioned a house on a small piece of land by the sea, just west of the Golden Gate Bridge. The cliff was very steep and Wright devised a plan that took advantage of the site by designing the tapered concrete pier that supports the end of the house.

The two glass rooms at the top of the tapered column gave 270° views of the surrounding terrain that included the Golden Gate Bridge that had been completed a few years earlier in 1937. The view was further enhanced by the placement of the building at the water's edge, with the adjacent buildings well back from the cliff, which from the road gave the impression that the house was only one storey high.

The Pittsburgh Point Project, Civic Center, Pittsburgh, Penn. (1947)

Edgar Kaufmann's first Wright design was for a weekend retreat in the mountains, 60 miles (100km) south-east of the city, the famous Fallingwater. Kaufmann was head of the largest department store in a booming city and had the best interests of the city in mind, and to this end he and Wright devised these plans to make the most of a difficult site where three rivers meet – often called the Golden Triangle. The scheme was an ambitious one and would have been very expensive to realize. The design encompassed an enormous ten-level spiral car park with two spiral ramps, so large that those who saw it doubted that it would ever be filled. However, they underestimated the popularity of the location which even now does not have this number of parking spaces.

It certainly made for an easy transition between the land and the river and included two bridges that spanned the

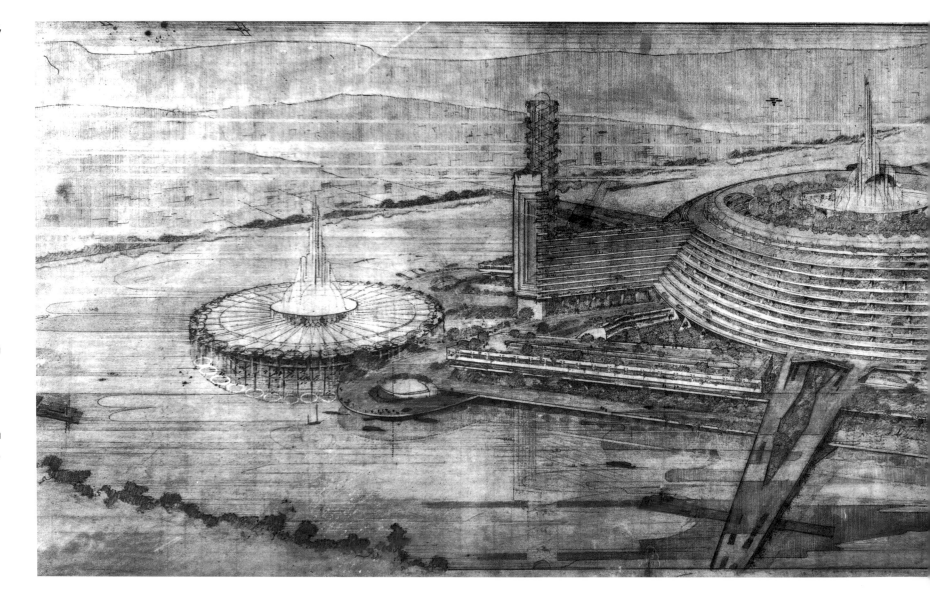

river and included several areas for planting to relieve the severity of the concrete used in construction.

There were several other Wright designs for Kaufmann and Pittsburgh: they included an apartment house designed for a steep lot that was originally developed for Elizabeth Noble on a similar site in Los Angeles, just a few years earlier in 1929. A second, smaller, circular parking garage was requested by Kaufmann for a site near the Kaufmann's department store, but was also unrealized.

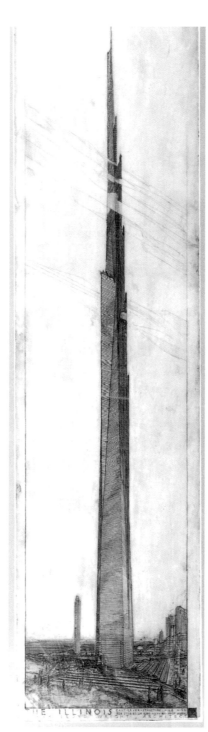

Mile High, Lincoln Park, Chicago, Ill. (1956)

Frank Lloyd Wright was due to be honoured by Mayor Richard J. Daley on 17 September 1956 and it was for part of this celebration that Wright presented his fantastic design. It was four times taller than anything that had been built up to that time, which was the Empire State Building in New York City. Even the drawing of the project was large, being over 25ft (7.6m) tall.

The building was shaped rather like an arrowhead and it was to be pointed to the west, to the prevailing winds. It was to have the very latest in futuristic facilities, such as landing pads for the many helicopters that would be bringing visitors to and from the building, and there was a large multi-level car park for lesser mortals.

Wright's idea was to concentrate the population in one place, leaving more open space available to view and enjoy. Within the city of Chicago, the building was to be located in what is now Lincoln Park, which is a large area situated along the shore of Lake Michigan, just 2 miles (3.2km) north of the city centre.

This design certainly captured the imagination of many people, including architects: even today, there are reports from manufacturers that they have only just achieved a level of technical development that would have made Mile High both possible and workable, and a major manufacturer has claimed that the latest elevators would have made life possible on all of the 528 floors that Wright had planned.

The Arthur Miller & Marilyn Monroe House, Roxbury, Conn. (1957)

This is an improvement and enlargement of a design executed several years earlier in 1949 for another client, Robert Windfoh, for a site in Fort Worth, Texas. Miller wrote of his encounter with Wright and was not especially flattering about it. It also appears that Monroe may have been the impetus and reason for the commission as she is thought to have visited Wright at his Plaza Hotel office several times in the preliminary stages of the project. There may have been a misconception on Wright's part when attempting to fullfil Miller's requirements, for Wright appears to have designed a much more elaborate building than was intended, which was rather more appropriate for Hollywood than Connecticut. In fact, Miller wanted a simpler, more traditional home rather than one geared to grand parties. The plan, however, did include a nursery, a hope that would never be realized though the site remains in Miller's possession. Miller and Wright did examine the property together to determine the most suitable site, Miller being greatly impressed by Wright's stamina at such an advanced age.

At the centre of the large circular living room was to be a glass dome, much like that of the Johnson Wax Administration Building, utilizing tubes as well as glass spheres set in cascades in several locations within the dome.

The building was never realized because the couple separated not long after the design was presented.

HOUSE FOR MR. AND M

FRANK LLOYD

ARTHUR MILLER

RIGHT ARCHITECT

CHAPTER SIX

Decorative Arts

The illustration is of the letterhead Wright designed at the time of the opening of his Oak Park Studio in 1897 and was on the brochure that he prepared and sent out. The red square was his signature mark for the first years of his independent practice after leaving Adler & Sullivan in 1893

FRANK·LLOYD·WRIGHT· ARCHITECT·▼·THE·ROOKERY·· CHICAGO·▼·ROOM·1119·▼·HOURS· TWELVE·TO·TWO·▼·TELEPHONE·MAIN·2668· DRAUGHTING·ROOMS·AND·STUDIO·AT·THE· CORNER·OF·FOREST·AND·CHICAGO·AVENUES· OAK·PARK·ILLINOIS·▼·HOURS·EIGHT·TO·ELEVEN A·M·SEVEN·TO·NINE·P·M·▼·TELEPHONE·OAK·PARK·

Frank Lloyd Wright has always been associated with the Arts & Crafts movement, which is as much due to his philosophy of clean, simple straight lines as to his choice of materials, in which oak predominates. In an attempt at expanding on the ideas of the British designer, William Morris, in 1901 Wright wrote and delivered a paper entitled 'The Art and Craft of the Machine', at the Hull House in Chicago. He took a more modern stance by championing the machine as a method of saving time and effort while still producing objects of beauty. Looking at Wright's work from another perspective, it may seem that he fits more comfortably into the category of art nouveau for several reasons. His was the New Art, although his lines were straight and were not an exemplification of the more familiar whiplash forms and sinuous curves associated with Horta and Guimard. Art nouveau was also a complete design concept, one that involved every item, not only of the architecture but also of the furniture and floor surfaces as well as the rugs which covered them. It dealt with other items encompassed by the so-called decorative arts such as art glass, lighting, carving and sculpture. Art nouveau was concerned with the arrangement and forms of plants, with cigarette cases, jewelry and even, or more especially, the clothing that the occupants of such interiors would wear. It was to be a completely integrated assemblage, with each item and each detail complementing and reinforcing the other. This is not to say that everything would be designed to death, as too often seen in 'coordinated' rooms, where the wallpaper is the same flower pattern and colour palette as the soft furnishings and the upholstery. This kind of room is both visually confusing and physically disorientating.

Decorative arts encompass a wide range of objects and designs. In Wright's case it includes furniture, art glass, lightscreens, graphics, metalwork, ceramics, as well as decorative architectural flourishes. Wright would, and did, design anything that was required, including women's clothing, and his approach was based on aesthetic principles rather than the 'look' of the moment, which is why his designs appear so timeless.

Wright had never been schooled in

either of the disciplines of furniture or graphic design but had an unerring feel for the processes and materials at his disposal and used their innate characteristics in the formulation of his designs. The historian Henry-Russell Hitchcock understood to the full Wright's marvellous talent which he thoroughly explores in his book, *In the Nature of Materials*.

The range of materials Wright used was broad: naturally he was familiar with the standard building materials regularly used by most architects of his day, those of brick and mortar, wooden boards, plaster and stucco. While these materials are historically the most common and have been used for millennia, Wright managed to utilize them in innovative and unusual ways without in any way altering their basic characteristics or deviating very far from what is suggested by the materials themselves.

In every case, Wright was not designing as an artist does, for his own satisfaction and amusement, or to make his work acceptable to a consumer, but with a specific client in mind and with the intention of fulfilling a specific request. The work was always directed to the client and not to himself. At the same time, Wright was also one of the greatest salesmen of all time and was more than capable of convincing clients that he knew best.

In these instances, Wright was therefore a designer rather than an artist in the normal sense of the word. He produced the designs and handed them over to someone else to execute – in fact, Wright never built any of his own designs, though he often worked closely with contractors whose bid was satisfactory. This was certainly the case with nearly all of his furniture. In the early or Prairie years, the drawings were tendered for competitive bid and later, in the Usonian era, most of the furniture was constructed by the finish carpenter engaged in the house construction. Moreover, the finishes and colours were approved by Wright even though they had been requested and required by the client; there were a wide range of wood finishes in the Prairie period – from clear to red mahogany through to walnut brown and almost black.

Wright's art glass was manufactured by a small group of specialized studios, some of which he visited, personally involving himself in the task of choosing individual sheets of glass that would be used in his designs; this was because the innovations Wright sought to reveal in his work required his own hands-on approach. Wright added a new dimension to the basic colour of the glass by having a layer of metal salts fired onto the surface which added a wonderful iridescence to the finished design.

All Wright's input into the decorative arts is based on strong geometric forms, the relationship of each piece or facet relating to the other in many unusual ways. Initially they are striking, and the more one looks at them, the more is revealed. However, the study of Wright's approach to the decorative arts has been sadly neglected, other than how it originated, by other artists and cultures.

PLATE 1 (ABOVE)
McArthur House entry
window

PLATE 2 (ABOVE RIGHT)
Blossom House entry hall
with sidelights

The Warren McArthur House, Chicago, Ill. (1892)

The model for this window pattern is most likely an ancient one – perhaps hundreds of years old. The circles are carefully placed with half-circles at all the edges. Wright modernized the design by adding a thin border around the sides. The small scale, though making the design most beautiful, must also have been quite expensive to manufacture.

The George Blossom House, Chicago, Ill. (1892)

The sidelights of this entry hall are based to a certain extent on Louis Sullivan's designs of only a few years earlier, interlocking circles being one of Sullivan's most common devices; however, the idea may have been developed by Wright himself when he was working at Adler & Sullivan. The fanlight above the door is a traditional design more

typically found in houses built several decades earlier. The windows have lead cames and clear, 1/4-inch (6.4-mm) plate glass.

Oak Park

Wright conceived and experimented with nearly every one of his early design ideas in his own home in Oak Park. However, despite his early interest in photography, there are few images of his early life. Many of his interests and hobbies had their beginnings in his Uncle Jenkin's All Souls Church when he arrived in Chicago in 1886 from Madison, Wisconsin. The term church was perhaps not completely accurate. Jones endeavoured to make all activities at the centre ones that were generally attractive and that would appeal to people of all ages.

House Beautiful

There was a very active microscopy and photographic club at All Souls Church, and while no roll was ever published of its members, Wright's prowess must surely have developed here, for at this time there are several photographs of the Jones Valley in Wisconsin taken by Wright and which he printed himself. There is also a series of photographs of wild flowers, published in the flyleaf of the publication for his client, William Winslow, the first *House Beautiful*, the text of this had been in print before, written by a close friend of Wright's Uncle Jenkin, William C. Gannet.

House Beautiful was designed by Wright. He provided the graphics for the title page as well as for the body of the book, designs which were often very elaborate and included detailed line drawings of fanciful geometric forms. Wright and Winslow produced all the copies on Winslow's printing press and it took them nearly two years to complete the project.

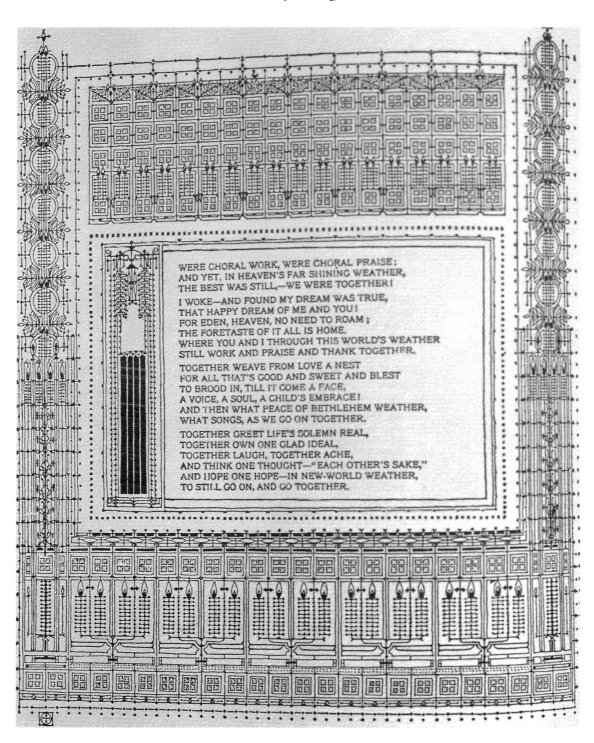

WERE CHORAL WORK, WERE CHORAL PRAISE;
AND YET, IN HEAVEN'S FAR SHINING WEATHER,
THE BEST WAS STILL,—WE WERE TOGETHER!

I WOKE—AND FOUND MY DREAM WAS TRUE,
THAT HAPPY DREAM OF ME AND YOU!
FOR EDEN, HEAVEN, NO NEED TO ROAM;
THE FORETASTE OF IT ALL IS HOME,
WHERE YOU AND I THROUGH THIS WORLD'S WEATHER
STILL WORK AND PRAISE AND THANK TOGETHER.

TOGETHER WEAVE FROM LOVE A NEST
FOR ALL THAT'S GOOD AND SWEET AND BLEST
TO BROOD IN, TILL IT COME A FACE,
A VOICE, A SOUL, A CHILD'S EMBRACE!
AND THEN WHAT PEACE OF BETHLEHEM WEATHER,
WHAT SONGS, AS WE GO ON TOGETHER.

TOGETHER GREET LIFE'S SOLEMN REAL,
TOGETHER OWN ONE GLAD IDEAL,
TOGETHER LAUGH, TOGETHER ACHE,
AND THINK ONE THOUGHT—"EACH OTHER'S SAKE,"
AND HOPE ONE HOPE—IN NEW-WORLD WEATHER,
TO STILL GO ON, AND GO TOGETHER.

PLATE 3
A page from *House Beautiful*, the text of which was originally by William C. Gannet

PLATE 4 (ABOVE)
Winslow House front door
carving

PLATE 5 (ABOVE RIGHT)
Winslow House: detail of
the decorative motif
surrounding the door frame

The William H. Winslow House, River Forest, Chicago, Ill. (1893)

The Winslow House was Wright's first recognized independent commission after leaving Adler & Sullivan. In it, there are clear allusions to design concepts attributable to Sullivan and which may have influenced Wright over several years, designs based on Sullivan's notion of a cotyledon, or seed pod. Wright continued developing what he had learned from Sullivan by simplifying and abstracting what attracted him, as can be seen in several examples at the Winslow House.

Winslow, along with his brother, owned the Winslow Brothers Iron Works which, within several years, would be casting very similar designs for Sullivan for the Carson building in downtown Chicago. It is all the more curious, therefore, that there is so little metalwork in Winslow's own house

The design on the front door **(Plate 4)** is of carved quarter-sawn white oak and the decoration surrounding it and the windows **(Plates 5 and 6)** are executed in limestone, the second-floor frieze being of gypsum plaster.

The oak-leaf flourish which appears on

the front door would not have been out of place on an Adler & Sullivan building it is so much in their style. The central element is the cotyledon, its stem or root emerging directly from it all the way to the base of the panel at the bottom rail.

In many ways the decorative devices evident in the Winslow House are unique; although the design of the stonework is a development of that which Wright was working on while employed at Adler & Sullivan. However, the patterns are more geometric than those of Sullivan's. The stone has been painted in such a way as to

370

highlight the grey of the limestone beneath, and the jams of the windows, the side surfaces, are also decorated, but with a pattern that differs from that which appears on the face.

There are no drawings of the Winslow furniture and few photographs of the original interior, so there is no absolute certainty that they are Wright's; but the designs are unusually simple and similar in many respects to his later designs. All of the furniture in the photographs appears to have been constructed from quarter-sawn white oak, though none of it is in the possession of the family and is presumed lost.

Two armchairs in the living room are exactly the same as two other pairs elsewhere, one in Wright's own house and the other in the foyer of Winslow's neighbour, Edward C. Waller **(PLATE 13)**. There is no direct evidence that they are Wright's, but given the advanced design and the fact that Wright was already designing his own furniture, it is very likely.

The table in the library **(PLATE 7)** is another possible Wright design, the use of quarter-sawn white oak and the broad, heavy legs being typical of Wright's other designs of the 1890s. The wallpaper, however, appears to be based on a Voysey design, the sinuous art noveau pattern appearing strikingly at odds with the severe rectangularity of Wright's later work.

PLATE 6
Winslow House entry with decorative motif surrounding the door frame

PLATE 7 (RIGHT)
Winslow library

PLATE 7 (RIGHT)
Winslow library

PLATE 8 (RIGHT)
Winslow hall

PLATE 9 (OPPOSITE ABOVE)
Winslow dining room

The arches set between the two doors in the entry **(PLATE 8)** develop the front door pattern by adding geometrical elements in much the same method as Sullivan had previously devised. The seats at either end are also likely to be Wright's because of the materials used, as well as the design of the upholstered seat cushion. The spindles on the left are as much a work of art as any decorative carved detail, with the clever inclusion of the interspersed thinner elements.

The glass patterns in the Winslow House derive from two sources, that in the front entry hall and in the second-floor windows seemingly metamorphosed from two Egyptian designs found in a German pattern book once owned by Wright; but those of the dining room bay window **(PLATE 9)** are clearly directly from Wright's drafting board. Both types were executed with lead cames and have mostly clear glass with small inset borders of blue glass.

The dining room is separated into two separate spaces by low walls at the entry to the circular bay. These walls have seats built into them and are emphasized at their junction with the wall by a set of oak columns with oak-leaf capitals. A window seat runs along the entire length of the round bay.

Winslow's house contained the work of several artists, and included Orlando Giannini's painting of a standing Native American.

acoustics, making conversation easier by reducing the distance the sound would have to travel. The red floor tile is set in a basket-weave pattern which is continued on the face of the fireplace at the end of the room. The walls were covered with a fabric that was similar in texture to that of a painter's canvas and coloured a soft brown.

Wright built his architectural studio and offices adjacent to his Oak Park house, the house being built in 1889 and the studio in

PLATE 10
Frank Lloyd Wright's Oak Park dining room

Frank Lloyd Wright's House, Oak Park, Chicago, Ill. (remodelled 1895)

The original kitchen of Wright's 1889 house was remodelled and expanded in 1895. An octagonal bay was extended out to the south and the ceiling was lowered to include a new ceiling light. Light bulbs were set against the original ceiling and below them Wright installed a pierced-wood grille, its pattern again being based on the work of his mentor, Sullivan. Behind the grille, Wright installed rice paper to diffuse the light over the dining table, the effect of which was of light filtering through tree branches, making the dining experience more like an outdoor picnic than a formal, traditional meal.

The furniture is Wright's own, the tall-backed chairs **(PLATE 10)** being among his earliest designs. This can be determined by the spindles that stop at the seat rather than continuing all the way to the floor, as in most other examples. The square spindles replaced helix spirals when the chairs were remodelled, as was the room itself. The dining table has a very large top that is 28 inches (71cm) from the floor – a departure from the more 'standard' 30 inches (76cm). The seat heights of the chairs are also 2 inches (5cm) lower. Wright did this to alter the apparent scale of the room and to make it appear larger than its dimensions. The lowered ceiling also altered the

PLATE 11 (RIGHT)
Moore House terra cotta
balusters

PLATE 12 (RIGHT)
Exterior decorative prism
plates manufactured by the
Luxfer Prism Company

PLATE 13 (OPPOSITE)
Waller House entry hall

1897. Both of these underwent almost continuous transitions until Wright moved out of the property in 1911. Wright also designed furniture for this building which included a series of spindle-box chairs comprising square spindles on three sides and arms with a rising arc toward the back and a tapered board across the top **(PLATE 16)**. A new type of adjustable table was also introduced at this time. Wright had long been a collector of Japanese prints and other works executed on paper and invented a special print table for the purpose of viewing them. The table has a reverse drop-leaf where the leaves fold up instead of down and form a portfolio pocket that drops into the frame. Four gate legs fold in, making the total width only 9 inches (23cm). The top can also be propped up on one side and the prints viewed in this way. The library once held another table, a more conventional one, that had a stationary top with octagonal legs and bun feet.

The Nathan G. Moore House, Oak Park, Chicago, Ill. (1895)

The flourishes on the undersides of the balusters shown in **PLATE 11** are almost Sullivanesque in their design. The terra cotta matched that used on the house and is also very similar to a design seen two years later, in 1897, for the Rolloson Row Houses in Chicago.

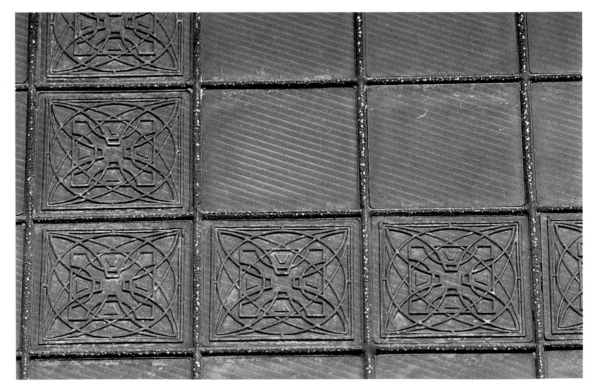

The Luxfer Prism Company (1897)

Wright produced the prism plate designs **(PLATE 12)** for his clients, William Winslow and Edward C. Waller, incorporators of the Luxfer Prism Company, later the American Luxfer Prism Company, formed by amalgamation with the American Prism Company several years after. The company expanded rapidly throughout the world after it was formed in 1897 in Chicago, and sets of prisms can often be found in the upper windows of commercial establishments built in the United States and Europe between 1898 and 1920.

Wright was always interested in the latest technology, as was his client and friend, Winslow, and it was Winslow's invention of 'electro-glazing' that made the process of assembling the plates worthwhile. Wright was hired as the architectural consultant and corporate representative liaising between the company and the architectural community.

The prism plates were used to alter the path of light as it entered a building and to redirect it further into the building, adding considerably to the usable area and allowing deeper floors in manufacturing and office buildings, a feature that was very important to architects of this type of construction.

The company sponsored a competition and Wright was asked to demonstrate in an elaborate form the use of prisms in a tall office building, his solution being to cover the street face of the building with square windows inset with clear central panels.

Wright's prism plate designs give some idea of the range of his graphics, though there is no indication that the surface designs altered or improved the performance of the prisms themselves. There are only two or three of the many prism plate designs ever produced and by far the most popular had a quatrefoil motif.

The Edward C. Waller House, River Forest, Chicago, Ill. (1899)

The Edward C. Waller House was originally designed by famed Chicago architect, Daniel Burnham. Wright was asked to remodel it and planned extensive work on the interior. On the second floor, above the entry hall, **(PLATE 13)**, is a large art-glass dome, while on the top of the newel post of the stairway that leads to the second-floor dome is a large and important copper urn. The urn was constructed by a Chicago firm that was also expert at making metal roofing and downspouts. They filled the base and the small domes on each of the four sides with fine sand which kept it upright and prevented unsightly dents from occurring. There were galvanized cylinders that acted as liners for each of these urns and they had an applied patina that gave them a reddish-brown tinge rather like a copper penny.

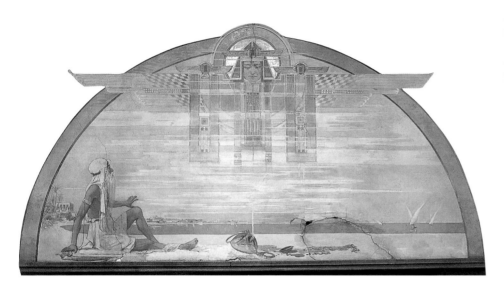

PLATE 14 (ABOVE)
Wright House playroom mural

PLATE 15 (ABOVE RIGHT)
Wright House tall-backed
spindled dining chairs

PLATE 16 (OPPOSITE ABOVE)
Frank LLoyd Wright's Studio,
with spindle box chairs

Frank Lloyd Wright's House & Studio

Wright built his Oak Park house in 1889 and enlarged it in 1895 with the addition of a large playroom with a new kitchen and pantry below. He added to the former kitchen by extending an octagonal bay out to the south and making it into the new dining room, for which he also designed new furniture.

Wright often made references to literature and philosophy in his work. He particularly enjoyed the *Arabian Nights* stories on which he based a mural painted on the end wall of the 1895 playroom addition in his Oak Park home **(PLATE 14)**. On very close examination, the artist did a fine job: the draftsmanship and the rendering of the figures is in fact excellent. There are several places that have been retouched with graphite and coloured pencils and are likely to be Wright's later handiwork rather than the original

artist's. At one time, the water of the lake extended past the right-hand border of the mural, all the way to the wall and another band connected at the top.

The tall-backed, spindled dining chairs **(PLATE 15)** were a major departure for Wright and may be the first dining chairs designed to be pulled up to the table and be seen from the back. Chairs were previously designed with their 'fancy work' showing on the front and were meant to be lined up along the wall. This is also why the front legs of traditional dining chairs have claw feet or other decoration and the back legs and feet are left plain.

The spindle-box chairs **(PLATE 16)** were

originally designed for the reception lobby of Wright's new 1897 Oak Park Studio. They are proportioned smaller than they appear in photographs but each part of the body is properly supported at each contact point.

The Joseph W. Husser House, Chicago, Ill. (1899)

The only image of an art-glass fireplace surround is the one in the Husser House **(PLATE 17)**. Wright also drew the wall that contained the fireplace and included a copper urn similar to the one featured in the Waller House and a large copper platter at the top of the upper mantle. The glass mosaic featured a wisteria motif with the

vines growing out of the ground on the left. This was the same motif that appeared in the D.D. Martin House of 1904 **(PLATE 48)** and the Ennis House of 1925 **(PLATE 107)**, and was installed by Orlando Giannini.

The Arthur Heurtley House, Oak Park, Ill. (1902)

The design of the dining room window below **(PLATE 18)** is an elaboration of the first windows Wright designed for the 1895 playroom addition to his own house, just a little way to the north of the Heurtley house. The different line thicknesses make it difficult to define the location of the actual border.

PLATE 17 (FAR LEFT)
Husser House art-glass fireplace surround

PLATE 18 (LEFT)
Heartley House window design

The Ward W. Willits House, Highland Park, Ill. (1901)

The Willits' dining room chairs **(PLATE 20)** came in two different heights, a tall-backed model and another with a lower back often called a medium-backed chair. The children of the family were quite small when the house was completed in 1902 and the Willits moved out of the house in 1952, long after the children had grown up. **PLATE 19** shows a medium-backed chair lifted by a small wooden frame. The height of this frame is equal to the difference in the height between the two chairs, thus making them the same height. It was the equivalent of putting a thick phone book underneath in order that a child might be seated at the proper height relative to the table-top. It was a great invention and also seems to be unique in Wright's career.

The armchair **(PLATE 21)** was designed several years after the spindle-box chair designed for the lobby of Wright's Studio **(PLATE 16)**, but it has some design features that would otherwise date it much earlier. One of these features is the parallelogram that frames the spindles on each side of the chair, which are not framed but dwindle away into the sides. The chair appeared in several early photographs of the living room **(PLATE 22)**.

The Francis W. Little House, Peoria, Ill. (1903)

Like the Willits House of 1901, the Little House had dining chairs of two different heights, tall- and medium-backed. However, unlike the Willits chairs, those of the Little house are missing the spindles often associated with Wright's chairs and have oak slats in their place, which gives a more solid appearance and also adds considerable weight to the two-piece tapered slat over the spindles **(PLATE 25)**. The original upholstery was leather in a colour amatching the wood stain.

The library table **(PLATE 23)** could be called the entertainments centre of its day and

PLATE 24 (LEFT)

Little House wall sconce

Letters from draftsmen in Wright's office suggest that Wright's assistant, Walter Burley Griffin, was the designer of this sconce, though it does not show up in any of his buildings. It was specified and installed in several of Wright's designs, and as well as the Dana and Little Houses, it was in the Heath House of Buffalo of several years later. Some of the lights were fashioned to accept a gas line at the top and an electric light bulb at the bottom, though most of them are fitted with a socket at both the top and the bottom. The frame is cast brass that incorporates eight rectangles of iridescent glass, darker on the face and more transparent on the sides. It is held by hooks attached to the square back plate.

held books, newspapers, cards and games.

Unlike the other pieces designed for the Little House, the console table **(PLATE 26)** is very heavy, both actually and visually, with the Y-legs at each end connected by a thick shelf. It is unlike any other Wright-designed furniture for the Little House or its nearby 'cousin' the Dana House.

One of the pieces Little moved from Peoria to to his later Wayzata house was a print table **(PLATE 27)**, which is identical to others found in Wright's Studio and the Dana House **(PLATE 42)**. In the Wright oeuvre, it is very unusual for designs used in more than one house to be as exactly similar as this.

The Susan Lawrence Dana House, Springfield, Ill. (1903)

Wright often referred to his stained-glass creations as 'lightscreens', which is an accurate term when applied to this hanging art-glass screen in the studio of the Dana House **(PLATE 28)**. The nine sections hang inside the half-round plate-glass window that keeps out the wind and rain, making it a lightscreen in every sense of the word. This is the only such installation in the Wright oeuvre.

The chair **(PLATE 29)** is a combination of two others: the spindle-box chair that Wright designed for his own Oak Park office **(PLATE 16)** provides the frame and the two unattached panels move to alter the pitch of the back in a Morris type of arrangement. The seat front lifts and pulls forward or pushes back into several set positions on dowels set into the top of the front stretcher. There were seat and back box pillows for added comfort.

This six-legged chair **(PLATE 30)** is architectural in concept in that it repeats the octagonal geometry of many of the bays used in several of Wright's 1890 and early 1900 houses. Another similar chair was designed and constructed for the Little House of Peoria at about the same time, though this octagonal-backed chair did not have the back two legs and the spindles cantilevered out to the back.

PLATE 25 (OPPOSITE LEFT)
Little House medium-backed chairs

PLATE 26 (OPPOSITE ABOVE RIGHT)
Little House console table

PLATE 27 (OPPOSITE BELOW RIGHT)
Little House print table

PLATE 28 (ABOVE LEFT)
Dana House studio glass lightscreen

PLATE 29 (FAR LEFT)
Dana House spindle-box recliner

PLATE 30 (LEFT)
Dana House octagonal-backed, six-legged chair

The window in **PLATE 31** is the uppermost portion of a design that extends through more than six separate windows on the east façade of the Dana House. The brick piers serve to make the window more architectural in spirit and they do not support any beam at the top. The straw-and-white base glass contains a fired metallic salt that causes it to become iridescent according to the light and the angle of view.

Another part of the overall pattern for the east façade can be seen below in **PLATE 32**. The glass used here is the same as that of the master bedroom window above the living room.

The nine individual art-glass panels are suspended inside the clear plate glass. This is what Wright often referred to when describing his unique window treatments – lightscreens. Many people are now taking antique art-glass windows and suspending them inside their own windows in ignorance of Wright's 1904 invention.

Between the three-storey space just inside the front door and the two-storey dining room is this low-ceilinged space that is also a part of the entry-reception area. In it are two features of particular importance, the first also being a feature unique to the Dana House – a fountain **(PLATE 33)**. It was modelled by Richard Bock and it is supposed that the models were Wright's own children. The fountain added much-needed humidity in the

winter along with the soothing sound of splashing water. It is constructed with a short brick base with a spout and terra cotta figures.

On either side and behind the fountain are doors and windows that contain the very best of Wright's art-glass designs. The cames are brass Colonial with iridescent, nearly transparent delicate milk glass and clear plate glass. (The glasswork of the D.D. Martin House had several added wisteria pendants flowing over and intertwining **(PLATE 48)**.)

These doors are located at the west end of the fernery and the front porch at the entry to the west studio space **(PLATE 34)**. In contrast to the fountain doors at the east end of the fernery, they are of a light and

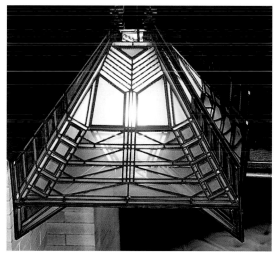

PLATES 35 and 36 (ABOVE)
Dana House dining room butterfly
hanging lights

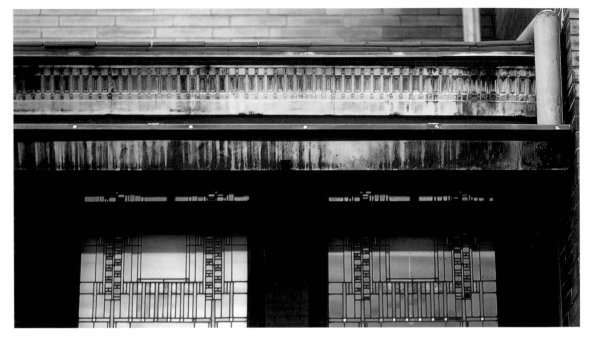

PLATE 37 (ABOVE)
Dana House double-pedestal
lamp

PLATE 38 (ABOVE RIGHT)
Porch window top

PLATE 39 (FAR RIGHT)
Music cabinet

PLATE 40 (OPPOSITE PAGE)
Drawing of the Dana House
entry hall

delicate design, originally flanked by silken drapes adorned with Japanese symbols.

Wright did not only design lightscreens in a flat plane but also in the form of art-glass hanging lights (**PLATES 35 and 36**), and independent free-standing models, some of which are the finest and most complex Wright ever produced. **PLATE 37** shows a double-pedestal table model which is covered by a hipped shade. There were two of this type and four of a single-pedestal design, most of which are in the house but have had the original applied patina removed, exposing a bright

shiny brass finish that is not in an altogether happy contrast to the rest of the building.

PLATE 38 demonstrates how Wright introduced decorative elements into practically every detail of the building, including the stamped copper gutters above.

For many years the music cabinet in **PLATE 39** (right) was understood to be a liquor cabinet, intended to house small glasses in the drawer at the top and decanters of port and brandy behind the fine art glass. There are small holes along the inside of the corners of the glass which are designed to hold the pins that support the glass shelves and the music that is stored on them. An elegant solution.

PLATE 41 (ABOVE)
Dana House square-legged table

PLATE 42 (ABOVE RIGHT)
Print table

PLATE 43 (RIGHT)
Back of sculptured figure

PLATE 44 (OPPOSITE LEFT)
Martin House bedroom window

PLATES 45 and 46 (OPPOSITE FAR LEFT)
Barton House window detail

PLATE 40 on the previous page provides a view of the interior arrangement impossible to obtain with a camera. It also presents a clear view of the vertical quality of the Dana House and provides an insight into the design of the furnishings as well as the anticipated location and disposition of them within the space.

The dining room is fitted with three separate square-legged tables (**PLATE 41**). Two are square and one is rectangular, which is often located between the other two. When the three tables were aligned with their leaves in place, they were able to seat almost 40 people. The legs are typical of Wright's table designs which lasted for about 20 years beginning with those of

Wright's own Oak Park house, as well as the tables to be seen in the library of the Winslow House (**PLATE 7**).

There are two examples of this print table (**PLATE 42**) in the Dana House and they are exactly like the one that was built for the Little House of Peoria and which was later moved to Francis Little's new house at Wayzata (**PLATE 95**), the living room of which was rebuilt in the Metropolitan Museum of Art in New York under the direction of Thomas A. Heinz.

A beautiful terra cotta sculpture (**PLATE 43**) greets visitors at the entry to the house. It is referred to as 'Flower in the Crannied Wall' because of the Tennyson poem inscribed on its reverse.

are over ¹/₂-inch (13-mm) thick and are brass double-crown Colonial. These were first introduced by the Chicago Metallic Corporation which is still producing them, along with the modern equivalent of the came, the 'T'-system for dropped ceilings that is so widespread in commercial interiors and offices.

This same pattern is also to be found in the Dana House. It was used in the porch doors and serves as the basis for the most resplendent of all of Wright's art-glass designs, the fountain doors in the lower-ceilinged entry next to the dining room **(PLATE 33)**. It is most unusual, especially at this time in Wright's career, for him to have used the same design in more than one building, but he must have been aware of the possibilities of utilizing this pattern as a basis on which to elaborate a theme in the Dana House.

The George Barton House, Buffalo, New York (1903)

PLATES 45 and 46 right show the inside and outside of the same window in a house which was actually built for Darwin D. Martin for his sister and brother-in-law, George Barton. The design, with a series of alternating lines of 45°-angle herring-bone, forms the centre of the flourish. The Heath House, also in Buffalo, has another of these examples.

The W. E. Martin House, Oak Park, Chicago, Ill. (1903)

The line weights of the window in **PLATE 44** above are more heavily contrasted than those of a similar pattern in the Heurtley House window **(PLATE 18)**. The tapering of the triple line as is passes the side borders is partly as a result of the addition of the white milk-glass squares. Here, the cames

The Darwin D. Martin House, Buffalo, New York (1904)

It was not until recently that the drawings for this chair **(PLATE 47)** were located and they confirm that the design for the entire piece was by Wright: earlier, it had been thought that only the quarter-sawn white oak base and legs were of his design. This is another example of Wright's desire to provide his clients with what they want. The footstool was a device from the past and was for the purpose of keeping one's feet up and away from cold floors. This stool, a carry-over from the Victorian era, of course, came before the invention and widespread use of central heating but, here again, with a simple accessory, Wright provides for the real and the perceived needs of his client. Mrs Martin had no real need of a footstool – Wright could have produced the same angle for the legs simply by making the chair a little lower. However, he gives the client what she thinks she needs at no real detriment to the result.

The art-glass mural that once covered all four sides of this two-way fireplace **(PLATE 48)**, and located between the entry hall and the living room, was one of the greatest works of art of Wright's career and it is through several acts of ignorance and neglect that we are now deprived of this treasure. The mural was one of only three that were ever installed in Wright buildings, the first dating from only five years earlier than the Martin House, in the 1899 Husser House of Chicago **(PLATE 17)**, demolished

in the 1920s, and the last in the Ennis House of Los Angeles **(PLATE 107)**. All had the same theme – a blooming wisteria vine, and all were nearly identical, apart from differences in size. All may have been installed, as well as made and produced by the talented artist, Orlando Giannini. The pendent flowers were in shades of blue, pink and white and the leaves were quite unusual in that they were cut and painted with a gold wash before refiring in an oven and allowed to cool slowly. As they cooled, the gold wash shrunk and separated, as mud dries. 'Alligatoring' is the term often used for this crackled effect, and the finish gives a variegated appearance to the leaves in much the same way as light dapples leaves in a garden. In the brochures of the Giannini & Hilgart art-glass firm, it states that this crackled gold process was patented – but no other such information appears to exist. The gold glass squares used as a background are identical in each of the three installations, as well as in several others of nearly identical designs by the Giannini firm.

There were several couches made for the Martin House of which this is one **(PLATE 49),** all of them having lines or sections of oak veneer. The radiused corners on the back of the arms are an unusual feature in an otherwise very square house. The yellow upholstery fabric is not original.

The tabouret has drawers and is perhaps more usable than the one designed for the Robie House **(PLATE 85)**, which is about the same size, but because of its utility, is much less elegant.

This section of glass **(PLATE 50)** is from a Los Angeles house built in about 1914. It was not designed by Wright but by some unknown architect and is nearly identical to the now-missing art-glass mosaic that once surrounded the two-sided fireplace at the entry to the D.D. Martin House **(PLATE 48)**.

PLATE 51 (RIGHT)

Green curtain and rug

PLATE 52 (BELOW)

The whereabouts of this dress has not yet been located, but it is believed to have been designed by Wright for Mrs Martin. There is at least one other dress which was worn by Wright's first wife, Catherine, and which is illustrated in photographs

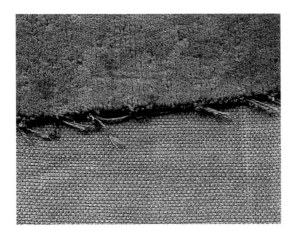

Above **(PLATE 51)** are samples of the original lime-green woollen rug and heavy silk draperies from the Martin House. They have only recently been discovered and impart a surprising splash of rich colour to an otherwise golden-brown interior.

PLATE 53 below shows a coffee-bean

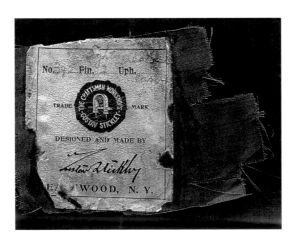

brown Oxford cloth fabric which once covered at least one of the several couches found at the Martin House. It shows at least

one of the popular sources for Arts & Crafts fabrics from just after the turn of the century. Wright sometimes specified Stickley furniture in some of his houses, for example, the Heath House, in Buffalo.

The table below **(PLATE 54)** is one of the finest of Wright's career; in fact there are actually two tables, if one counts the independent inset shelves as one. The gently radiused corners soften the severity of the geometry as does the sweeping line at the base.

The first design for the chair opposite **(PLATE 55)** and the way it was originally built was as a T-base in plan. This same geometry of a three-pointed base for a chair was used many years later for the secretary's chair at Johnson Wax in 1936 **(PLATE 111)**. Martin revealed, in his great collection of letters and diaries, that he considered the design unsuitable and had the chairs altered to this four-legged version as it now exists.

This chair below (**PLATE 56**) is one of the finest of all Wright's furniture designs. In it, the proportions and use of materials are ideal, the entire frame being constructed in solid oak as well as the solid curved back. The back is constructed from a laminated but solid block of oak with a compound curve that could only be carved. The curve of the back is different from that of the front and the curve of the top of the arm fits the underside of the arm at just the right point, making it one of Wright's most comfortable chairs.

PLATE 53 (OPPOSITE CENTRE BELOW)
Original label on brown fabric

PLATE 54 (OPPOSITE RIGHT)
Great table

PLATE 55 (LEFT)
Dining chair

PLATE 56 (BELOW)
Barrel chair

PLATE 57 (BELOW)
Larkin desk

PLATE 58 (BELOW RIGHT)
Desk with chair unfolded
This is the view of the chair
unfolded ready for use. The
desk is shown in its original
colours

**Larkin Company Administration
Building, Buffalo, New York (1903)**
This contains some of the first metal office
furniture ever produced – in fact, many
firsts occurred with the construction of the
Larkin Building, including wall-hung
lavatories. The desk **(PLATE 57)** was also
paired with metal filing cabinets. The chair
is attached to the leg of the desk and was

able to adjust up and down according to
the needs of the occupant. The angle of the
back could also be adjusted by inserting a
pin into any one of a number of holes in
the ratchet. The back of the chair pivoted in
and out off the leg **(PLATE 58)**. The back
folded down and could be tucked into the
kneehole after hours to make it easier for
the office to be cleaned.

Wright's inventiveness did not go
unremarked. While his design and
specifications could be complicated, and
much patience was required by the different
subcontractors, in the end, they seemed
pleased with the work that they executed for
Wright and his clients. The management of
the Van Doren Iron Works were very pleased
indeed and showed off their work in a half-

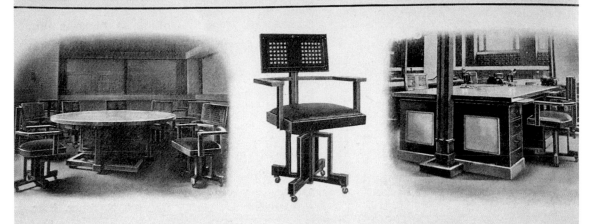

The Architectural Record. 11 East 24th Street, New Y

FRANK LLOYD WRIGHT

esigned the steel furniture equipment for Larkin Company, w
was manufactured by

PLATE 59 (FAR LEFT)
Advertisement by the Van
Doren ironworks, producers of
metal furniture for the Larkin
Building

PLATE 60 (LEFT)
Drawing of the entry fountain
in the Larkin Building

PLATE 61 (LEFT)
Executive swivel chair

page advertisement **(PLATE 59)** in a national architectural magazine. It is curious that Wright did not turn to his friend and client William Winslow for such a commission.

Though the Larkin building was demolished in 1950, there were several important decorative details that should not be overlooked. The fountain **(PLATE 60)** at the entrance to the building was an unusual feature for Wright to have introduced in an office building. It was not intended to be merely a series of pools with water gurgling between them; instead, Wright devised that a sheet of water should fall into a square basin, while above the spout was a

decorative plaque designed by Wright and his collaborator, Richard Bock.

The swivel chair **(PLATE 61)** was designed to accommodate a wide range of body sizes. The flat back pivots from a pin at the centre of the panel to rest at any angle. There is a knob at the centre of the four legs which raises and lowers the height of the seat. The arms are of wood and the leather seat is heavily padded for comfort. The base is cast and the remainder of the pieces are constructed of folded steel.

PLATE 62 (RIGHT)

Cheney House living room

window

PLATE 63 (FAR RIGHT)

Rear hall window

The Edwin H. Cheney House, Oak Park, Chicago, Ill. (1904)

Wright transposed his use of variations in the line weight into this delicate design for Edwin and Mamah Cheney's living room **(PLATE 62)**. The squares at the upper third point of the window are made from the same stock of straw cathedral glass as many of Wright's other fine windows and has a wonderful quality of iridescence about it. Wright applied several sets of subtle borders to these window patterns.

When a bedroom hallway is distant from the outside walls, there is little chance of a window providing it with any light. This would normally be true, but not in a Wright house. Wright introduced a light shaft, painted white for maximum light transference, through the centre of the chimney mass and provided a window **(PLATE 63)** to flood the hall with daylight. The sandblasted glass not only blocks the view of the painted brick but also diffuses more light into the hall.

The Smith Bank, Dwight, Ill. (1905)

Wright was interested in geometry, so it is natural that he should design round-backed chairs, such as the classic barrel chair of the Darwin D. Martin House of 1904 **(PLATE 56)**. The Smith Bank chair **(PLATE 64)** of the following year is another but less successful attempt. It has a bent-wood back and the seat and stretchers are also rounded; but the total integration of the design is much less successful than in the Martin House example. The other odd feature is the

inset at the outside edges of the top rail. There is no apparent reason for this and it detracts from the nature of the wood used at this position. The vertical back is curious in the way that it drops from the arm rail and ends below the seat at the circular stretcher.

The W.A. Glasner House, Glencoe, Ill. (1905)

The Glasner House has two octagonal rooms, a sewing room on the north side and a library at the east overlooking the street

front: this window **(PLATE 65)** is from the library. Each of the seven sides once faced a white oak tree set on the centre line of the window, which may account for the blank in the centre of the window pattern, a location which nature was meant to fill. The two linear patterns at the edges of the window measure two-thirds of the sidelights for the larger living room windows. The pattern appears unique and not derivative of any other.

Many have said that the patterns in the

window in **PLATE 66** symbolize the traditional 'tree of life' device that appears in so many cultures. However, it is more likely, since Wright was a Unitarian, that it is merely an abstraction of a plant form used in so many of his lightscreens. Traditional tree-of-life patterns have 12 branches but this one has 14.

PLATE 64 (ABOVE FAR LEFT LEFT)
Smith Bank round chairs

PLATE 65 (ABOVE CENTRE)
Glasner House library window

PLATE 66 (ABOVE)
Exterior iridescent window

PLATE 67 (RIGHT)
Beachy House tall-backed
dining chair

PLATE 68 (FAR RIGHT)
Unity Temple decorative
columns

PLATE 69 (OPPOSITE)
Boynton House dining room

**The P.A. Beachy House, Oak Park,
Chicago, Ill. (1906)**
This tall-backed dining room chair (**PLATE
67**) is probably the plainest of all of
Wright's 20 or so such chair designs. The
rear legs are tapered from the seat to the
top and again from the seat to the floor.
The front legs are straight, as is the seat.
Unlike the Dana House chairs (**PLATE 33**),
there is no trim around the seat rails or
anywhere else. This design still manages to
embody elegance while retaining the utmost
simplicity of form.

Unity Temple, Oak Park, Chicago, Ill. (1906)

Wright designed the Unity Temple with many kinds of economy in mind. One of these was to make duplications in several areas of the building and to this end he used the same forms for all the columns on all eight elevations where they appear. The capitals **(PLATE 68)** contain the same squares and rectangles used in so many of Wright's decorative elements.

The E.E. Boynton House, Rochester, New York (1908)

Like the Dana House dining room, the Boynton House **(PLATE 69)** has more than one dining set, and a larger and a smaller table. There are also two heights of dining chairs as has been seen in the Little and the Willits houses **(PLATES 20 and 25)**. The larger table is illuminated at the top of the outboard legs as Wright disliked hanging chandeliers and the lights determined the centre of the table that was to be set below them. This did not allow for variations in the placement of the furniture. The three ceiling lights took the place of the chandelier in providing light by which to dine.

Upon closer inspection, the tall-backed dining chairs are not exactly vertical, as in most of the other examples, but are canted back just a little. This did not seem to have affected their comfort.

Art Institute of Chicago (1906–1918)

There were several exhibits of Wright's collections at this museum between the above two dates. The two black-and-white photographs **(PLATES 71 and 72)** are from an exhibition of part of Wright's Japanese print collection, which even at this time was sizeable and important. It is obvious that Wright mounted and installed the prints on the walls of the exhibition rooms, as well as providing some of his original art to be placed upon the pedestals throughout, though it is unlikely that the bench came from or was approved by him. Wright was said to have one of the largest and finest collections of Japanese Ukioye

PLATE 70 (ABOVE)
Print stand

PLATES 71 and 72 (ABOVE
RIGHT and RIGHT)
Interior of Japanese print
show

wood-block prints outside of Japan. He even included some fine screens to span the space between some of the taller pilasters.

The print stand opposite **(PLATE 70)** was designed around the same time as the Midway Gardens project and is discussed in correspondence between Wright and his second son, John, who assisted in the design. The area at the top of the piece was proportioned with dimensions to accommodate certain prints that were made during the Edo period. The design appears simple but is in fact quite complex. The base is supported at the centre and below the horizontal base by a small vertical brace. The spindles stop at this shelf but the frame that holds them and the print above, passes the shelf and returns well below the brace.

The Avery Coonley House, Riverside, Ill. (1908)

The Coonley House is one of Wright's greatest interiors and he was able to complete nearly everything that he intended for the house, except for the dining room furniture. This included the rugs, draperies, table runners, wall murals, and nearly all the other furniture designs, including those for the living room and the bedrooms. While there were many other buildings with

Wright-designed furniture, this was one of the few to have Wright's rug designs. The significance of these is that so few were designed and fewer still were actually woven and installed. Not many have the original full-sized drawings, watercolours and yarn samples that make it possible to reproduce them when required.

Archive material illustrates how Wright was able to carry out his philosophy of total integration. The colours of the living room rugs **(PLATES 73 and 74)** reflect

those used throughout the Coonley house, the golden-brown border matching the stain used on the wooden trim. The centre field of the rug is the colour of sheepskin, a neutral beige, the same shade as all the ceilings throughout the house. The square motifs contain green, blue and red, the colours of the walls in the living room, bedrooms and dining room respectively. The bright green exactly matches the colour of the cathedral glass in the art-glass windows.

PLATE 73

Coonley House old living room

PLATE 74 (RIGHT)
Coonley House hall, linking
the living and dining rooms

PLATE 75 (FAR RIGHT)
Drawing of tall-backed chair

PLATE 76 (BELOW)
Rug sample

PLATE 77 (OPPOSITE ABOVE
LEFT)
Desk design for the rear guest
room of the Coonley house

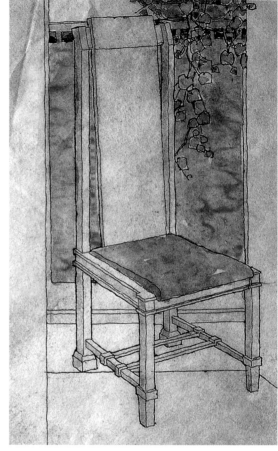

The drawing of a tall-backed chair
above **(PLATE 75)**, is of a type that would
have been presented to a client and then,
once approved, would have been
developed into a working drawing before
tender and construction.

(PLATE 76) left shows a reproduction
rug based on original yarn samples and full-
sized drawings found in the Niedecken &
Wallbridge collection of Milwaukee's Prairie
Archive.

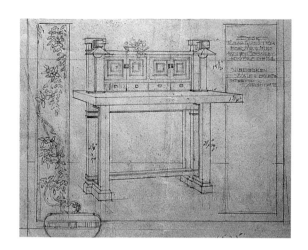

There are no photographs of this desk **(PLATE 77)** in its original location in the Coonley guest room. The desk was approved and constructed and is now in the collection of Chicago's Art Institute. It is one of the few pieces of free-standing furniture to be electrified for the two small sconces at either side of the doors and is one of the most beautifully proportioned pieces in the Wright oeuvre.

The Isabel Roberts House, River Forest, Ill. (1908)

Wright designed several of the reclining chairs shown in **PLATE 78** for many of his houses. Each had the same base dimensions and had a unique method for adjusting the angle of the back of the chair. Inside the basic frame are two loose panels, one for the seat and one for the back. There were box pillows for both the seat and the back which

could be added for extra comfort.

The other variations were all made of oak and had spindles or panels. The panels were sometimes vertical, sometimes horizontal – even framed as in the William E. Martin House of Oak Park, where there were two built-in examples on the third floor.

Isabel Roberts worked in Wright's office during the Prairie years, as well as for Hermann von Holst when he took over the office during Wright's trip to Europe in 1909. Afterwards she worked with Marion Mahony and Walter Burley Griffin. Her origins are unclear but she was an architect and designed many buildings and this wonderful house was designed while she was employed by Wright. She is mistakenly thought to be the daughter of another Wright client of the same name, Charles E. Roberts of Oak Park.

The interior is one of the best. Along with it came a full suite of newly designed furniture built in curly fir rather than quarter-sawn white oak. The rugs in the photograph **(PLATE 79)** are simple, as are the other furnishings. On the upper right deck, above the fine collection of books, is a Teco vase designed by Hugh Garden for the Northwestern Terra Cotta Company of Chicago and owned by William Gates.

Years later, an owner attempted to improve upon Wright's design but was eventually forced to call on Wright for help

in the remodelling which included a brick resurfacing, a new copper roof and built-in cabinet work in the dining room.

PLATE 78 (BELOW LEFT)
Roberts House recliner

PLATE 79 (BELOW)
Old living room with recliner, side chair, dining chair and rug

PLATE 80 (RIGHT)
Browne's Bookstore tall-
backed chairs

PLATE 81 (OPPOSITE LEFT)
Robie House old living room

PLATES 82 and 83 (OPPOSITE
RIGHT, ABOVE and BELOW)
Front and back views of tall
chair

Browne's Bookstore, Chicago, Ill. (1908)
It was once thought that the chairs in
PLATE 80 had been lost when the small
bookshop was closed and demolished many
years ago. However, they fortunately turned
up at Unity Temple in Oak Park with no
evidence of their provenance. They are
taller than most of Wright's other tall-backed
chairs, perhaps in contrast to the small but
tall space Wright created in the Fine Arts
Building on Chicago's Michigan Avenue, just
north of Sullivan's Auditorium Building. The
seats are square and flat, perhaps intended
to be used only for a short time and
certainly not for dining.

**The Frederick C. Robie House, Chicago,
Ill. (1909)**
The Robie House was the second complete
interior Wright designed after the Coonley
House of the previous year. Here, as in
that house, Wright designed almost
everything – the furniture, the lighting, the
table runners – as well as the rugs (at least
on the main floor). Most of the furniture has
been accounted for except for the large
library table **(PLATE 81)** near the centre of
the photograph.

PLATES 82 and 83 (opposite far right)

show different views of the most unusual of Wright's tall-backed chairs. It has an upholstered back and a solid wood, framed panel on the reverse. There is another such chair with upholstered back designed for the Bradley House of 1900 which has also been referred to as 'The Cardinal's Chair' because of the red velvet fabric and the stately height of the its back.

The watercolour on the left **(PLATE 84)** is part of a very large collection discovered by Brian A. Spencer, a Wisconsin architect. The Niedecken & Wallbridge company was often used by Wright to execute his decorative devices and there is some indication that they may have also assisted in the design of some of the pieces. Also in the Niedecken & Wallbridge collection are the original yarn samples and in many cases, full-sized drawings for the rugs. These are very rare and are a good indication of the now lost colour record.

Left **(PLATE 85)**, is one of the most perfectly proportioned pieces of Wright's career. The stool/tabouret was used as what today would be a coffee or more correctly a tea table and at the Robie House was tucked under the cantilever of the special couch designed for the living room.

The slant-backed chair on the right **(PLATE 86)**, is probably the most universal of Wright's furniture designs. There were hundreds produced for the Larkin Company

dining room and examples were also to be found in Wright's own Oak Park house as well as in the Unity Temple. In each location there were variations: tapered versus square seats and blocks onto and at the bottom of

the legs. A few examples have the back tapered from top to bottom. The diagonal of the back added considerably to the strength of the piece as well as relieving the severity of the right-angles.

The living room doors in **PLATE 87** (above) open onto the front or south balcony of the house; the balcony is not very wide and would be crowded if any furniture were to be brought onto it. The art-glass pattern seems to stop about halfway down from the top of the doors. This may have been as part of a cost-saving exercise since the bottom half would not have been seen from the street and one would naturally assume that the pattern continued all the way to the bottom.

PLATE 88 (BELOW)

Taliesin bedroom with stone walls

PLATE 89 (RIGHT)

Early bedroom with two single beds

PLATE 90 (OPPOSITE)

The earliest living room

Taliesin I, Spring Green, Wisc. (1911)
The bedroom in **PLATE 88** (below) is located behind the stone wall of the living room/dining area and has a higher ceiling than that of the living room. The fireplace to the right is still used and this eventually became Olgivanna Wright's bedroom after the death of her husband in 1959. The stonework throughout Taliesin is some of the best of Wright's career. The same pillows which appear in other Taliesin bedrooms of this era are shown on the bed and the pattern extends onto the back of the upholstered armchair to the right. The ceiling is trimmed in the same manner as the living room and above the bed is another six-panelled Japanese screen.

Another bedroom, this time with two single beds set very close to one another **(PLATE 89)**, is from the same earliest years of Taliesin. The beds are certainly Wright designs and utilize a simple fir footboard framed with a 2-inch (5-cm) edging. The large pillows decorated with embroidered circles is a recurrent theme in all of the bedrooms.

Opposite **(PLATE 90)** is perhaps the earliest photograph of the living room of the new building at Taliesin in the Jones Valley, built in about 1911 by Wright for himself and Mamah Borthwick Cheney after their return from Europe. The furnishings are quite striking, with several animal skins adorning the furniture. All of the lighting is from gas fixtures, as electricity was

apparently not extended into the valley until many years later. The furniture upholstery is in a checkerboard pattern, very similar to that used in the Imperial Hotel several years later. There are three tall print stands that were designed for Wright's Japanese print show at the Art Institute of Chicago several years earlier **(PLATE 70)**. The low dining table at the centre of the photograph is flanked by benches on either side and a very wide chair at the end. A five-panelled Japanese screen is on the lower wall behind the table with a cabinet above, the doors of which are cut from a single piece of timber.

Perhaps the most interesting part of the room is the ceiling: there is a dark band above the wood-trimmed headline that is further framed onto the flat upper ceiling, connected to the headband at the inside corners or reverse hips. At each junction is an even darker accent, squares at the top and triangles at the bottom. This same system was used by Wright in the living room of the Aline Barnsdall House of California, better known as the Hollyhock House.

PLATE 91 (RIGHT)
Taliesin armchairs and floor lamps

PLATE 92 (OPPOSITE LEFT)
1911 Oak Park dining chair

PLATE 93 (OPPOSITE RIGHT)
Single beds with tall headboards

In an unidentified room at Taliesin **(PLATE 91)** is an arrangement that includes armchairs that are copies of the one at the end of the dining table in the living room **(PLATE 90)**. The centre chair, however, is a narrower version and was probably designed for this specific arrangement. The tall floor lamps have never been seen and are the predecessor of those of the Booth House of 1915. It would appear that raw silk shades the bulbs and diffuses the light emitted by them.

Wright's House & Studio, Oak Park, Wisc. (1911)

Wright remodelled his 1889 house and 1897 studio when he abandoned his family to move into Taliesin with Mamah Borthwick Cheney in 1911. The chair opposite **(PLATE 92)** is one of the designs he executed for this remodelling and is more elegant than earlier chairs of the type, the high stretchers and overhanging seat contributing greatly to its appearance. They were intended for Wright's private office that was later converted into a dining room for his family.

The single beds in **PLATE 93** have octagonal cantilevers at the top of the tall headboards. Unfortunately, it had not been taken into account that parents would most likely hit their heads when saying goodnight to their children. Similar beds were designed and built for the Sherman Booth

House of 1915. The Indian squaw above the beds was painted by one of Wright's favourite artists, Orlando Giannini, who was fond of portraying Native Americans.

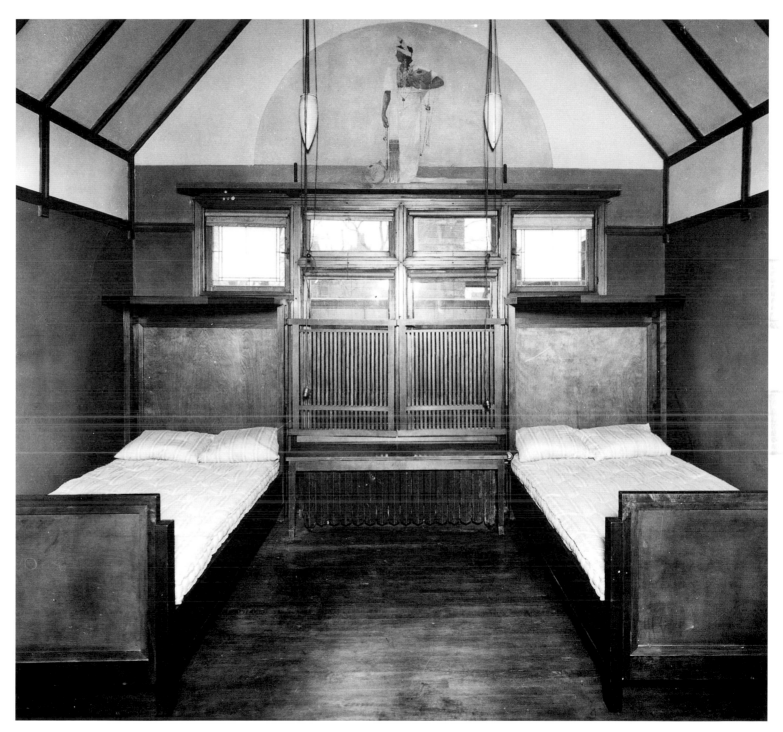

The Avery Coonley Playhouse, Riverside, Ill. (1912)

This view **(PLATE 94)** is of the original configuration of the building with its original art-glass windows. The three in the centre are worthy of particular note. Often they are shown with the colours brightly shining – a rare view while they remained in the building. The glass used is flashed, in this case constructed from two layers of different coloured glass. There was a white base glass that faced the street and another, with primary colours of red, blue, green, yellow and orange. These colours are flashed over the white based glass and considerably soften the effect and intensity of the colour making it nearly pastel. This is the reason why all the large circles appear to be the same colour – they are the same colour from this point of view. Most of the impact of the windows to the side is lost in this photograph because of the shading of the roof overhangs. This would have made the impact of the lively patterns much greater and more of a surprise and a delight for the children who habitually visited it.

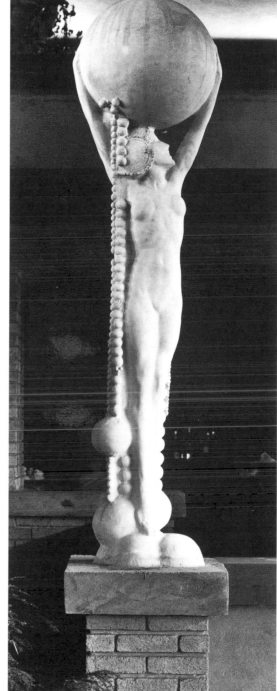

Francis W. Little House, Wayzata, Minn. (1913)

Francis Little had previously lived in a house Wright had designed for him in Peoria before he moved to the Minneapolis, Minnesota area. He wrote to Wright during a summer in Pasadena, California requesting a design for property he had purchased on a lake west of Minneapolis in Wayzata. Wright designed a very long house, set on a rise overlooking a 2-acre (0.8-hectare) plot to the south and Lake Minnetonka to the north. Little's daughter eventually sold the house to the Metropolitan Museum of Art in New York who had it dismantled, crated and moved to their warehouse in New York. Thomas A. Heinz was hired ten years later as restoration architect to rebuild it inside the new American Wing.

Wright designed very little new furniture for this new house, built in 1913. However, this cantilevered console table **(PLATE 95)** is such an example. It is not made from quarter-sawn oak but of a less figured wood, possibly Douglas fir. The design is much more abstract than earlier designs and there is no metal hardware apart from rectangular finger holes to open the cabinet doors. Above the cabinet is a shelf. This piece is now tucked into a corner of the reconstructed room.

Midway Gardens, Chicago, Ill. (1914)

PLATES 96 and 97 (right) show the two extremes of the sculpture Wright devised with his collaborator Alfonso Ianelli of the eight or so examples used at Midway Gardens. The scale of all the figures is about the same from one example to the other. The female figure with the

PLATE 98 (RIGHT)
Imperial Hotel porcelain

PLATE 99 (BELOW)
Silverware

bubbles, balloons and beads reflects the circle in three dimensions and the outside figure holding the two cubes represents the square. The pole lamp behind the outside figure is constructed of metal and glass with 11 light bulbs, one for each of the light cubes. The cubes are open at the top to allow the hot air to escape.

The Imperial Hotel, Tokyo, Japan (1916–1922)

Wright was willing to design just about anything that was suggested to him or that had been requested by a client. He designed this china service **(PLATE 98)** for the grill of the Imperial Hotel, its pattern

based on recurring, superimposed circles.

A fine hotel designed to attract Westerners would have had room service and liquid refreshments would certainly have been on offer, which would have included tea, coffee and hot cocoa. Wright designed a tea and coffee service for the Imperial Hotel but only one piece seems to have survived the wars and economic circumstances of the years and it was later owned by Wright and his wife. However, an important Pasadena collector later

discovered a 17-piece service complete with sugar tongs in a sale in southern California, which includes coffee and teapots of different sizes, creamers and milk pitchers, as well as brown and white sugar bowls. They are inscribed with an overlapping 'IH' on one of the faces of their octagonal sides **(PLATE 99)**. There are no known examples in drawings or in actuality of any silver sets of knives, forks and spoons made for the hotel or other locations.

The Frederick C. Bogk House, Milwaukee, Wisc. (1916)

The table opposite **(PLATE 100)** is one of the finest of the furniture designs of Wright's middle period, 1910–1935. Wright's cantilever is emphatic here and the asymmetrical balance of the mass below the top adds to its interest and appeal. It also reinforces the cantilever above the suspended cabinet at the right side of the table. The line of squares on the edge of the top are of inlaid ebony, lying flush with the adjacent surfaces. There is a line of ebony about 2 inches (5cm) inboard of the edge framing the surface. The centre drawer can be opened from either side. As in earlier, similar pieces, this was the entertainments centre of the house before the advent of television and computers. The mahogany used for the Bogk furniture and building trim is a client-requested departure from most of Wright's other work of this and his earlier Prairie period.

PLATE 101 shows one of Wright's few complete dining rooms of the second decade of the 20th century. The sideboard has its original lighting as well as built-in Japanese prints along its top.

PLATE 100 (LEFT)
Bogk House library table

PLATE 101 (BELOW)
Bogk dining room

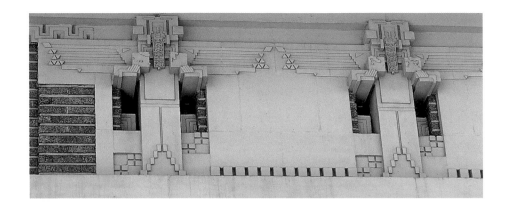

There are no other large-scale sculptures on any of Wright's residential designs. Here, high on the façade of the Bogk house **(PLATE 102)**, is a frieze of abstract figures with outstretched arms holding blocks in their hands. There may or may not be stylized wings behind the figures, while beneath their arms are deep-set windows that illuminate the attic.

Below **(PLATE 103)** are some of the few caned furniture pieces of Wright's career and are rather more conventionally designed than most of Wright's other dining room chairs. Perhaps one of their most interesting and consistent features is that the caned panel of the back passes the seat, as do the spindles and panels of Wright's tall-backed chairs.

PLATE 102 (ABOVE)
Bogk House façade frieze detail

PLATE 103 (RIGHT)
Dining room chairs

The Aline Barnsdall (Hollyhock) House, Los Angeles, Calif. (1920)

PLATE 105 shows samples of the original fabrics used at the Barnsdall or Hollyhock House in Los Angeles. The velvet is purple with the tips of the fabric fading to a grey-brown and then diamond-cut.

The Alice Millard House (La Miniatura), Pasadena, Calif. (1923)

Wright had left the Prairie era far behind him by the 1920s and had developed a new outlook. He designed a series of houses, large and small, in the Los Angeles area and the first was the second design for an earlier client, Alice Millard. Wright helped her choose a site in fashionable Pasadena, just north of Los Angeles, which was a site that most developers would have shunned, consisting as it did of a ravine rather than the usual square, flat site that more commonly found approval with builders. Wright felt that these unusual natural features would give his design a unique character and it certainly did.

The Millard House was constructed of 16-inch square (41-cm²) concrete blocks of Wright's design **(PLATE 104)**, which were stacked one upon the other and were patterned; where Wright needed a window or other ventilation, the incised lines and figures were allowed to pierce the block completely. The glass was added behind the block, as in this case, where the four blocks at the centre of the wall are thus pierced.

PLATE 104 (LEFT)
The Alice Millard House: detail of concrete block system of construction

PLATE 105 (ABOVE)
Samples of fabrics used in Aline Barnsdall's 'Hollyhock House'.

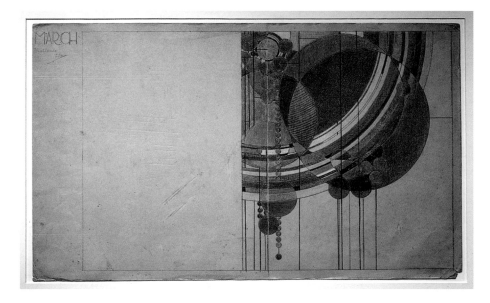

Cover Design for *Liberty* Magazine

Wright was not faring all that well in the 1920s, but he was able to obtain a commission for the design of 12 monthly covers for the magazine *Liberty*. Wright's grasp of graphics was wide-ranging and he designed and hand-drafted all of the designs himself. Each month had a different but relevant theme, icicles in winter and fruit from the orchard in summer. July had a wonderful series of American flags of differing sizes and abstractions which was later used as a cover for *Town & Country* magazine.

Above, in **PLATE 106**, is the cover for the month of March known as 'Balloons'. No one is quite clear why the two should be so associated but the cover is certainly most attractive.

The Charles Ennis House, Los Angeles, Calif. (1924)

The Ennis House was the last of Wright's houses to have lightscreens, or art-glass windows fitted **(PLATE 107)**. It, like the earlier Millard House, was constructed of square concrete blocks which influenced the design of the glass patterns. It appears that the Judson Studios installed and manufactured the art glass and the wisteria mosaic and are still in business in Los Angeles where they are a flourishing company which not only creates new work but also consults on older installations and restorations.

Darwin D. Martin House (Graycliff), Derby, New York (1927)

Wright designed very few buildings and even less furniture in the 1920s, even though the economy was prospering; but one of them was for Darwin D. Martin and his wife Isabelle and was situated on several acres of land on the shore of Lake Erie, south of Buffalo. The design has many features which were developed for Taliesin, including stonework and stucco. It is, however, a more formal structure than Taliesin and is also open to the public for tours.

The furniture bears some resemblance to that designed for the Imperial Hotel which was completed just a few years earlier. The legs of the table in **PLATE 108** (above right)

consist of boards set at angles to one another rather than a square, thick piece. The wood is not oak because the house was designed to be used as a summer home.

The S.C. Johnson & Son, Inc. Administration Building, (Johnson Wax) Racine, Wisc. (1936–1939)

The large dome opposite **(PLATE 109)** is constructed from hundreds of simple concentric circles of Pyrex tubing. The rows of circles above these form the supporting structure for the dome in a fashion somewhat reminiscent of the dome of the Guggenheim Museum, New York many years later. This dome is located on the second floor of the first building Wright designed for the Johnson Wax Company in 1936 and accentuates the entry way to the executive offices as original planning indicated. The wood for the casework was American walnut, unusual in Wright's career where, for 70 years, he had predominantly used oak.

Wright introduced tremendous variety into the design of the glass tubes and considered many different aspects that would have been overlooked by lesser designers. The photograph in **PLATE 110** (right) shows the bridge that connects the executive offices with the main workroom, the ceiling of which is barrel-vaulted with the tubes set longitudinally. The glass walls relieve any feeling of claustrophobia that one might expect to experience in such a long and narrow hallway. The many reflections contribute to this feeling of openness.

Wright was concerned with economy, both in financial terms and in the use of materials. This also applied to the expenditure of energy or motion. The steel, three-legged chair in **PLATE 111** (below) is a case in point. The steel tubes are welded at their joints and the rounded back is able to pivot all the way round, actually turning the back to the front. It is the same size at the seat and the face panel of the back can be substituted for the seat in the event of it wearing out or being damaged; many of the chairs had brass shoes instead of wheeled casters. Wright understood the importance of economy in motion, in this case, when typing or using an adding machine and felt, along with Johnson, that good posture was an important part of the equation. The chair's three legs required the occupant to keep both feet firmly on the floor or face tipping the chair back. However, in these current litigious times this would plainly not do, and most of the chairs have been altered to include a more stable fourth leg.

The Edgar Kaufmann House (Fallingwater), Mill Run, Penn. (1936)

Above the entry and to the side of the stream, Mill Run, is the guest room. Each of the rooms in Fallingwater have custom-designed shelves, cabinets and closets for storage. The guest room **(PLATE 112)** has a built-in desk opposite the built-in bed illuminated by a Wright-designed light equipped with several bulbs beneath a horizontal wooden shade, and there is a cast metal base. The shade can be easily

adjusted to produce direct or indirect light. The built-ins are all veneered with American walnut.

When Wright designed furniture, the process was usually followed by a plan showing the size and suggested location of each piece. This was originally the case for the room below **(PLATE 113)**, but as the owners lived in the house for many years,

they naturally imposed their own taste on it, altering Wright's vision in the process. However, in this photograph, the living room furniture is arranged the way Wright intended. The house's overall concept, of overlapping and cantilevered elements, is carried through in the differing heights of the tables and seating and is much more formal than Kaufmann's subsequent rearrangement.

Wright designed a series of tables like the one in **PLATE 114**, all with differing heights and all based on a unit system which determined their proportions. They do not consist of quarter-sawn oak but of walnut veneers with half-rounded caps to the edges of the plywood. The boards are slipped into slots as in an egg-crate and topped with a square.

PLATE 113 (BELOW LEFT)
Fallingwater living room furniture set

PLATE 114 (BELOW)
Tall little table

The Stanley Rosenbaum House, Florence, Ala. (1939)

Wright spent most of his last 20 years exploring the possibilities of using plywood in his furniture, as it has great tensile strength and can also be used with larger solid members as a stable structural membrane or diaphragm. Here, at the Rosenbaum House **(PLATE 116)**, he designed the dining chairs to use as little material as possible. The seat of the chair is canted to the back and the angle of the chair-back is set for the seat height,

PLATE 115 (ABOVE)
Wingspread dining room set with barrel chairs

Plate 116 (RIGHT)
Rosenbaum House dining set

The Herbert F. Johnson House (Wingspread), Racine, Wisc. (1937)

Wright was always experimenting and the dining table for Wingspread **(PLATE 115)** was no exception. The original intention was that the entire table could be pulled through the wall and fully into the kitchen at the end of each course. This, naturally, would have left the diners sitting in their chairs looking at an empty space and sadly without their glasses of wine. Johnson did not find this at all satisfactory, so the table was extended, not by means of leaves set into the top, but by adding smaller tables complete with bases clipped onto the end. There were several located throughout the house like end tables that would be set up depending on the number of guests.

The barrel chairs are adaptations of those from the 1904 Darwin D. Martin House in Buffalo **(PLATE 56)**, though these versions are executed in plywood that was bent to produce the curved backs. The arms are straight and thinner than the Martin example and are also slightly narrower.

something Wright carefully studied so that the occupants would be as comfortable as possible. Above the table are three shelves that are built into the horizontal joints of the woodwork and are in keeping with the modular concepts he developed in these later houses.

Wright's Lincoln Automobile

Wright was quick to see opportunities where others only saw disaster. One of his 1939 Lincoln automobiles (**PLATE 117**) was involved in a roll-over accident in which the roof was crushed, so Wright decided to redesign the car to his own taste which included a pair of semi-circular windows flanking the sides of the rear seat. At the same time he also had it repainted in his favourite colour which came to be known as Cherokee or Taliesin red. The car can be seen at the Stevens Plantation, also called Auldbrass, in South Carolina.

PLATE 117
Frank LLoyd Wright's redesigned and repainted Lincoln automobile

PLATE 118 (RIGHT)

Lewis House pole lamp

PLATE 119 (FAR RIGHT)

Taliesin West music stand

PLATE 120 (OPPOSITE)

The 'Olgivanna' chair

The Lloyd Lewis House, Libertyville, Ill. (1940)

Wright considered the way rooms were lit to be one of the most important features of any building, and designed this beautiful pole lamp **(PLATE 118)** as an accent piece which is at the same time also a sculpture. The simple wooden boxes and reflectors are assembled in such a way as to emit interesting light effects.

Taliesin West, Scottsdale, Ariz. (1938)

Music played an important part in the life of the Taliesin Fellowship and Wright designed this music stand **(PLATE 119)** that could accommodate as many as six players at a time. Another of these was built for the Zimmermans of Manchester, New Hampshire, who were also music-lovers and who liked to have a string quartet or other ensemble to play to guests in their living room.

In the Taliesin archives there is a wonderful drawing of this innovative design, which is known as the 'Olgivanna' chair **(PLATE 120)**, presumably because it was for Wright's last wife. It is constructed from a series of ¼-inch (6.4-mm) thick strips of plywood glued to small ¼-inch spacers set side by side and which give it considerable strength and style.

Butterfly Chair

Wright loved Japonaiserie and especially origami, or objects made from folded paper, which were his particular favourites. This chair combines this fascination with his interest in plywood to produce a chair which is quite comfortable even though it looks rather ungainly. This example **(PLATE 121)** is constructed from mahogany plywood, but others of this type are of common fir plywood.

Pope-Leighy House, Woodlawn, Va. (1940)

Perfect simplicity is very difficult to achieve. The table on the right **(PLATE 122)** is an example of Wright's quest for inexpensive designs for his less costly houses. There was

a series of other, smaller, tables that could be lined up and attached to this main table when guests were expected, and at other times set at different locations around the living room.

Exhibition House Tall-Backed Chair

Wright continued to develop the uses of plywood in the example in **PLATE 123** from the Exhibition House that once stood on the site of the Guggenheim Museum. As with much of Wright's furniture, at first glance it appears to be quite simple but on closer inspection is rather more complex. In this case, the seat is interlocked with the back and the base has one side wider than the other. When they were on display in the Exhibition House, both the seat and back were fitted with box pillows and the plywood edges were coloured red.

The David Wright House, Phoenix, Ariz. (1950)

Alternative furniture arrangements were very important to Wright and he designed these hexagonal tables **(PLATE 124)** to be used in groups to allow for greater flexibility. They could also be used singly. The small shelf below the top fits modern lifestyles very well now that we have remote controls, cell phones and other small but important electronic devices at our disposal.

PLATE 123 (LEFT)
Exhibition House tall-backed chair

PLATE 124 (ABOVE)
David Wright House hexagonal table

PLATE 125 (BELOW)
Christian House chair with TV
tray

PLATE 126 (RIGHT)
Living room

**The Dr. John E. Christian House,
Lafayette, Ind. (1954)**

Television was very new in the early 1950s,
but Wright seemed to be well aware of the
lifestyle changes these inventions would
bring. He designed this TV table **(PLATE
125)** for Dr. Christian and his family, the top
being a simple tray that can be easily
removed. The base comprises two boards
hinged at the front and enables the table to
be folded and stored away. It is light enough
to be easily moved at a moment's notice.

The living room coffee table **(PLATE
126)** is actually a series of alternating
triangular-topped tables set in a row which
can be redistributed around the room as the
occasion warrants. Similar tables were
designed for the Heritage-Henredon line
that became available to the public a year
or so following the appearance of these
designs. The stools could also be used for
extra seating when the Christians were
entertaining. Examples of similar stools are
to be found in many of the Usonian houses.

**The P.A. Beachy House, Oak Park, Ill.
(1906), The Lovness House, Minneapolis,
Minn. (1955)**

The two chairs in **PLATE 127** amply illustrate
the evolution of Wright's tall-backed dining
chairs. They were designed 50 years apart,
one for the Beachy House of Oak Park (see
also **PLATE 67**) and the other, more modern
one, for the Lovness House of Minneapolis in
1955. They are striking in both their
differences and their similarities. The Beachy
House example on the right is constructed of

solid quarter-sawn oak with square spindles spanning the space between the bottom stretcher and the top rail, set in a row between the back legs which taper in two directions. It has an upholstered seat with a lapped frame below and webbing stretched over the frame.

The Lovness chair (left) is constructed of ¼-inch (6.4-mm) thick mahogany plywood for the back and ¾-inch (19-mm) plywood for the seat and base. The seat has a box pillow filled with foam that rests on top of the seat.

One of the most interesting points is that over the 50 years which separate these designs, Wright changed neither the 16-inch (41-cm) seat height, nor the height of the spindles.

The Isaac Newton Hagan House, Ohiopyle, Penn. (1954)

The famous painter, Claude Monet, considered that a work could not be regarded as art unless it was signed. Wright felt just as strongly about his own work and signed many of his later examples with a square red tile inscribed with his initials **(PLATE 128)**. This example appears on the Hagan House, built just a few miles from Fallingwater, and which is also open to the public.

PLATE 127 (LEFT)
The Beachy chair (right) and the Lovness chair (left), two chair designs separated by 50 years

PLATE 128 (ABOVE)
The square red tile which was Wright's signature

PLATE 129 (ABOVE)
Heritage-Henredon coffee
tables

PLATE 130 (BELOW)
Taliesin colour palette in
Martin-Senour paints

PLATE 131 (OPPOSITE PAGE)
Heritage-Henredon dining set

The Heritage-Henredon Range of Furniture (PLATES 129 and 131)

Wright was convinced that the furniture designs he had produced for individual clients who used his architectural services would also be of interest to a wider market. This turned out not to be the case and was possibly because the designs he was now producing were a marked departure from what had gone before. There were carvings along the edges as well as stone tops for some of the tables which had not been an earlier feature of Wright's private designs, and had the work not been so strikingly different, it may indeed have proved to have been more successful.

Some of the pieces, in the form of the smaller tables and benches, have nevertheless become popular in auction

rooms, and there are a few bedroom sets and sideboards. The green slate tops seem to quite a large degree to add to the designs.

Martin-Senour Paints (PLATE 130)

Little is known of Wright's use of colour because most of his original schemes have been overpainted by insensitive and ill-informed owners over the course of many years. What little is known of the original colours is apparent from this colour card Wright assembled in the 1950s and shows the ones he used most frquently in his long career. However, not every colour is represented and was not intended to be, but it is a good guide for people nowadays working on their Wright interiors. A second card was issued in the 1990s but many of the colours were altered and several failed to appear at all.

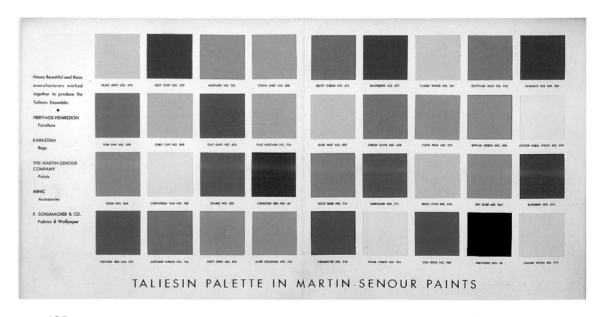

TALIESIN PALETTE IN MARTIN-SENOUR PAINTS

1885 All Souls Church, Chicago, Illinois

1886 Unity Chapel, Spring Green, Wisconsin

1886–89 Auditorium Building, Chicago, Illinois

1887 Hillside Home School I, Spring Green, Wisconsin

1889 Frank Lloyd Wright's House, Oak Park, Illinois

1891 James Charnley House, Chicago, Illinois

1892 George Blossom House, Chicago, Illinois

Robert G. Emmond House, La Grange, Illinois

Warren McArthur House, Chicago, Illinois

Robert P. Parker House, Oak Park, Illinois

1893 Walter Gale House, Oak Park, Illinois

William H. Winslow House, River Forest, Illinois

Francis J. Woolley House, Oak Park, Illinois

1894 Robert W. Roloson Row Houses, Chicago, Illinois

1895 Francisco Terrace, Chicago, Illinois

Nathan G. Moore House, Oak Park, Illinois

Waller Apartments, Chicago, Illinois

Chauncey L. Williams House, River Forest, Illinois

Harrison P.. Young House, Oak Park, Illinois

1896 Harry C. Goodrich House, Oak Park, Illinois

Isidor Heller House, Chicago, Illinois

Charles E. Roberts House, Oak Park, Illinois

Romeo and Juliet Windmill, Spring Green, Wisconsin

George W. Smith House, Oak Park, Illinois

1897 Frank Lloyd Wright's Studio, Oak Park, Illinois

George and Rollin Furbeck Houses, Oak Park, Illinois

1900 William Adams House, Chicago, Illinois

B. Harley Bradley House, Kankakee, Illinois

Stephen A. Foster House, Chicago, Illinois

Warren Hickox House, Kankakee, Illinois

Fred B. Jones House, Delavan, Wisconsin

E.H. Pitkin House, Sapper Island, Desbarats, Ontario, Canada

Henry Wallis House, Delavan, Wisconsin

1901 E. Arthur Davenport House, River Forest, Illinois

William G. Fricke House, Oak Park, Illinois

F.B. Henderson House, Elmhurst, Illinois

Frank W. Thomas House, Oak Park, Illinois

Ward W. Willits House, Highland Park, Illinois

1902
George and Walter Gerts Houses, Whitehall, Michigan

Arthur Heartley House, Oak Park, Illinois

Arthur Heartley Cottage, Marquette Island, Michigan

Hillside Home School II, Spring Green, Wisconsin

Charles S. Ross House, Delavan, Wisconsin

George W. Spencer House, Delavan, Wisconsin

1903
Abraham Lincoln Center, Chicago, Illinois

George Barton House, Buffalo, New York

Susan Lawrence Dana House, Springfield, Illinois

Warren H. Freeman House, Hinsdale, Illinois

Horse Show Association Fountain, Oak Park, Illinois

Larkin Company Building, Buffalo, New York

Francis W. Little House I, Peoria, Illinois

William E. Martin House, Oak Park, Illinois

1904
J.J. Walser House, Chicago, Illinois

Edwin H. Cheney House, Oak Park, Illinois

Robert M. Lamp House, Madison, Wisconsin

Darwin D. Martin House, Buffalo, New York

1905
Mary M.W. Adams House, Highland Park, Illinois

Hiram Baldwin House, Kenilworth, Illinois

Charles E. Brown House, Evanston, Illinois

E-Z Polish Company, Chicago, Illinois

William A. Glasner House, Glencoe, Illinois

Thomas P. Hardy House, Racine, Wisconsin

William R. Heath House, Buffalo, New York

A.P. Johnson House, Delavan, Wisconsin

Rookery Building, Chicago, Illinois

Smith Bank, Dwight, Illinois

1906
Peter A. Beachy House, Oak Park, Illinois

K.C. DeRhodes House, South Bend, Indiana

A. W. Gridley House, Batavia, Illinois

P.D. Hoyt House, Geneva, Illinois

George Madison Millard House, Highland Park, Illinois

Frederick D. Nicholas House, Flossmoor, Illinois

Pettit Memorial Chapel, Belvidere, Illinois

River Forest Tennis Club, Illinois

Unity Temple, Oak Park, Illinois

1907
George Fabyan House, Geneva, Illinois

Stephen M.B. Hunt House I, La Grange, Illinois

Andrew T. Porter House, Spring Green, Wisconsin

Harvey P. Sutton House, McCook, Nebraska

Ferdinand F. Tomek House, Riverside, Illinois

Burton J. Westcott House, Springfield, Ohio

1908
E.E. Boynton House, Rochester, New York

1943   Herbert Jacobs House II, Middleton, Wisconsin

1943–56   Solomon T. Guggenheim Museum, New York City

1944   Johnson Wax Administration Building Research Tower, Racine, Wisconsin

1945   Lowell Walter House, Quasqueton, Iowa

Watson Administrative Building, Florida Southern College, Lakeland, Florida

1946   Douglas Grant House, Cedar Rapids, Iowa

Chauncey L. Griggs House, Tacoma, Washington

Alvin Miller House, Charles City, Iowa

1947   Amy Alpaugh House, Northport, Michigan

A.H. Bubilian House, Rochester, Minnesota

Unitarian Church, Shorewood Hills, Wisconsin

1948   Albert Adelman House, Fox Point, Wisconsin

Caroll Alsop House, Oskaloosa, Iowa

Erling Brauner House, Okemos, Michigan

Maynard P. Buehler House, Orinda, California

Jack Lamberson House, Oskaloosa, Iowa

Morris Gift Shop, San Francisco, California

Eric Pratt House, Galesburg, Michigan

David I. Weisblatt House, Galesburg, Michigan

Charles Welzheimer House, Oberlin, Ohio

Robert D. Winn House, Kalamazoo, Michigan

1949   Howard E. Anthony House, Benton Harbor, Michigan

Eric V. Brown House, Kalamazoo, Michigan

James Edwards House, Okemos, Michigan

Samuel Eppstein House, Galesburg, Michigan

Sol Friedman House, Pleasantville, New York

Kenneth Laurent House, Rockford, Illinois

Robert Levin House, Kalamazoo, Michigan

Ward McCartney House, Kalamazoo, Michigan

Herman T. Mossberg House, South Bend, Indiana

Edward Serlin House, Pleasantville, New York

Melvin Maxwell Smith House, Bloomfield Hills, Michigan

1950   Robert Berger House, San Anselmo, California

Raymond Carlson House, Phoenix, Arizona

Richard Davis House, Marion, Indiana

First Christian Church, Phoenix, Arizona

John A. Gillin House, Dallas, Texas

Thomas Keys House, Rochester, Minnesota

Arthur C. Mathews House, Atherton, California

Curtis Meyer House, Galesburg, Michigan

Robert Muirhead House, Plato Center, Illinois

Henry J. Neils House, Minneapolis, Minnesota

William Palmer House, Ann Arbor, Michigan

Donald Schaberg House, Okemos, Michigan

Seymour Shavin House, Chattanooga, Tennessee

David Wright House, Phoenix, Arizona

1951 Benjamin Adelman House, Phoenix, Arizona

Gabrielle & Charlcy Austin House, Greenville, South Carolina

A.K. Chahroudi Cottage, Lake Mahopac, New York

S.P. Elam House, Austin, Minnesota

Herbert F. Glore House, Lake Forest, Illinois

John Haynes House Fort Wayne, Indiana

Patrick Kinney House, Lancaster, Wisconsin

Roland Reisley House, Pleasantville, New York

Nathan Rubin House, Canton, Ohio

Karl A. Staley House, North Madison, Ohio

Mrs Clinton Walker House, Carmel, California

1952 Anderton Court Shops, Beverly Hills, California

Quintin Blair House, Cody, Wyoming

Ray Z. Brandes House, Issaquah, Washington

Andrew B. Cooke House, Virginia Beach, Virginia

Price Company Tower, Bartlesville, Oklahoma

Archie B. Teater House, Bliss, Idaho

Isadore J. Zimmerman House, Manchester, New Hampshire

1953 Jorgine Boomer House, Phoenix, Arizona

Louis Penfield House, Willoughby Hills, Ohio

Frank Sander House, Stamford, Connecticut

Robert L. Wright House, Bethesda, Maryland

1954 E. Clarke Arnold House, Columbus, Wisconsin

Beth Sholom Synagogue, Elkins Park, Pennsylvania

John E. Christian House, West Lafayette, Indiana

Danforth Chapel, Florida Southern College, Lakeland, Florida

John J. Dobkins House, Canton, Ohio

Ellis A. Feiman House, Canton, Ohio

Louis B. Frederick House, Barrington Hills, Illinois

Maurice Greenberg House, Dousman, Wisconsin

Willard H. Keland House, Racine, Wisconsin

Isaac Newton Hagan House, Ohiopyle, Pennsylvania

Harold Price Snr. House, Phoenix, Arizona

Harold Price Jnr. House, Bartlesville, Oklahoma

William L. Thaxton House, Houston, Texas

Abraham Wilson House, Millstone,
New Jersey

1955   Dallas Theater Center, Dallas, Texas

Randall Fawcett House, Los Banos,
California

Maximillian Hoffmann House, Rye,
New York

Toufic Kalil House, Manchester,
New Hampshire

Donald Lovness House, Stillwater,
Minnesota

Theodore A. Pappas House, St.
Louis, Missouri

John L. Rayward House, New
Canaan, Connecticut

Gerald B. Tonkens House, Amberly
Village, Ohio

William Tracy House, Normandy
Park, Washington

Dorothy Turkel House, Detroit,
Michigan

1956   Annunciation Greek Orthodox
Church, Wauwatosa, Wisconsin

Frank Bott House, Kansas City,
Missouri

FLW Foundation Visitors' Center
(Riverview Terrace Restaurant),
Spring Green, Wisconsin

Allen Friedman House,
Bannockburn, Illinois

Kundert Medical Clinic, San Luis
Obispo, California

Meyers Medical Clinic, Dayton,
Ohio

Eugene Van Tamlen House,
Madison, Wisconsin

1957   Al Borah House, Barrington Hills,
Illinois

Donald Duncan House, Lisle,
Illinois

Fasbender Medical Clinic, Hastings,
Minnesota

Conrad E. Gordon House,
Wilsonville, Oregon

Frank Iber House, Plover, Wisconsin

Arnold Jackson House, Madison,
Wisconsin

Juvenile Cultural Center, Wichita,
Kansas

Lindholm Service Station, Cloquet,
Minnesota

James B. McBean House, Rochester,
Minnesota

Rudin House, Madison, Wisconsin

Carl Schultz House, St. Joseph,
Michigan

Robert G. Walton House, Modesto,
California

Wyoming Valley School, Spring
Green, Wisconsin

1957–66   Marin County Civic Center, San
Rafael, California

1958   George Ablin House, Bakersfield,
California

Lockridge Medical Clinic, Whitefish,
Montana

Paul Olfelt House, St. Louis Park,
Minnesota

Seth Peterson Cottage, Lake Delton,
Wisconsin

Pilgrim Church, Redding, California

Donald Stromquist House,
Bountiful, Utah

Duey Wright House, Wasau,
Wisconsin

1959   Grady Gammage Memorial
Auditorium, Tempe, Arizona

Ina Morris Harper House, St.
Joseph, Michigan

Richard Smith House, Jefferson, Wisconsin

J.A. Sweeton House, Cherry Hill, New Jersey

1961   Socrates Zaferiou House, Blauvelt, New York

1966   Norman Lykes House, Phoenix, Arizona

Unrealized Projects

1895   Luxfer Prism Company Skyscraper, Chicago, Illinois

1907   Harold McCormick House, Los Angeles, California

1911   Sherman M. Booth House, Glencoe, Illinois

1921   Edward H. Doheney Ranch, Los Angeles, California

1924   National Life Insurance Company, Chicago, Illinois

1929   St. Mark's-in-the-Bowerie, New York

1945   Daphne Funeral Home, San Francisco, California

V.C. Morris House (Seacliff), San Francisco, California

1947   Pittsburgh Point, Pittsburgh, Pennsylvania

1956   Mile High, Lincoln Park, Chicago, Illinois

1957   Arthur Miller & Marilyn Monroe House, Roxbury, Connecticut

List of Plates in Chapter Six

PLATE 1   McArthur House entry window

PLATE 2   Blossom House entry hall with sidelights

PLATE 3   A page from *House Beautiful*

PLATE 4   Winslow House front door carving

PLATE 5   Winslow House: detail of the decorative motif surrounding the door frame

PLATE 6   Willits House: decorative motif surrounding the door frame

PLATE 7   Winslow House library

PLATE 8   Winslow House hall

PLATE 9   Winslow House dining room

PLATE 10   Frank Lloyd Wright's Oak Park dining room

PLATE 11   Moore House terra cotta balusters

PLATE 12   Exterior decorative prism plates manufactured by the Luxfer Prism Company

PLATE 13   Waller House entry hall

PLATE 14   Wright House playroom mural

PLATE 15   Wright House tall-backed spindled dining chairs

PLATE 16   Frank Lloyd Wright's Studio, with spindle box chairs

PLATE 17   Husser House art-glass fireplace surround

Notes on Text

Joseph Lyman Silsbee and the Shingle Style

Silsbee was the first architect the young Frank Lloyd Wright met through his uncle Jenkin Lloyd Jones and the building of All Souls Church in Chicago and the Unity Chapel in the Jones Valley, where Wright was thought to have assisted in the design. Silsbee was well known for using shingles to cover both roofs and external walls and the style was the first strong architectural influence Wright received.

Louis Sullivan

Sullivan, a partner in Adler & Sullivan, had a rich decorative style possibly developed from John Ruskin, a proponent of the value of ornamentation in architecture. He was greatly revered by Wright who regarded him as his mentor.

Ladies' Home Journal

Wright became nationally well known toward the end of the 19th century through his contribution to this journal, notably 'A Home in a Prairie Town', published in 1901. Its purpose was to demonstrate that inexpensive houses could be built while still retaining individuality and character. Succeeding designs included a square concrete house and a fireproof plan in 1907.

Prairie Style

This was exemplified in the *Ladies' Home Journal* designs in the form of low pitched roofs with wide overhanging eaves which Wright considered to be the embodiment of the real spirit of the American West and Midwest. The Prairie houses were horizontal in form, often of one storey, and with the rooms flowing into one another in a continuous space. Large fireplaces were centrally placed to emphasize their position at the heart of the home.

Usonian (United States of North America) Houses

In the 1930s Wright introduced his Usonian House designs which brought into being new developments in the building of inexpensive structures, particularly pre-cast concrete. This was radically different from his earlier Prairie Style and favoured flat roofs and a blurring of the division between the inside and outside worlds through the use of large areas of plate glass. More flexibility was introduced into the interiors with the addition of movable screens instead of fixed room walls. Herbert Jacob's first house could be said to be the prototype of the style of which hundreds were built, not all of them by Frank Lloyd Wright.

Concrete Block System

From 1917 to about 1924 Frank Lloyd Wright was in California where he designed a number of important houses including La Miniatura and the Charles Ennis House in which he used his new exposed textile block system. The poured concrete blocks were reinforced with metal rods and were decorated on both sides. These could be omitted in places to allow the passage of light into the house and the spaces were sometimes glazed.

**Photographic and Picture
Acknowledgements**

All photographs are supplied copyright © **Thomas A.
Heinz** with the exception of those on pages 8, 9, 16,
17, 20, 28, 34, 35, 37, 41 which are **Courtesy The
Frank Lloyd Wright Archives, Scottsdale, Arizona**:
the drawings on pages 27, 33, 38–39, 358, 359, 360,
361, 362, 363, 364–365 which are **Copyright ©2000
The Frank Lloyd Wright Foundation, Scottsdale,
Arizona**: page 388 (left) which is courtesy the
**University Archives, State University of New York,
Buffalo**: page 395 (PLATE 64) which is courtesy
Michael Fitzsimmons Decorative Arts: page 398
(both black-and-white photographs) which are courtesy
the **Art Institute of Chicago** (Japanese Print
Exhibition): page 417 (both) which are courtesy
Johnson Wax: page 420 (right) which is courtesy
H.-R. Hitchcock: and page 429 which is by courtesy of
Butterfields.